When a Woman Chooses to Forgive

Cheryl Brodersen

HARVEST HOUSE PUBLISHERS
EUGENE, OREGON

WHEN A WOMAN CHOOSES TO FORGIVE

Copyright © 2014 by Cheryl Brodersen
Published by Harvest House Publishers
Eugene, Oregon 97402
www.harvesthousepublishers.com

Library of Congress Cataloging-in-Publication Data
Brodersen, Cheryl, 1960-
When a woman chooses to forgive / Cheryl Brodersen.
pages cm
ISBN 978-0-7369-5596-6 (pbk.)
ISBN 978-0-7369-5597-3 (eBook)
1. Christian women—Religious life. 2. Forgiveness—Religious aspects—Christianity.
3. Forgiveness of sin. I. Title.
BV4527.B738 2014
241'.4—dc23
2013014358

Printed in the United States of America

16 17 18 19 20 21 22 / BP-JH / 10 9 8 7 6 5 4 3 2

Acknowledgments

I would like to dedicate this book to my heavenly Father, who has forgiven us every sin and wrongdoing through the blood of Jesus Christ.

Special thanks to all those who entrusted me with their precious testimonies of transformation and forgiveness.

I also want to express my profound appreciation to my husband, Brian, who continually showers me with grace and forgiveness.

I am grateful for the amazing mentoring and tender kindnesses of my editor, Hope Lyda.

May God be glorified!

Contents

The Life-Changing Choice

What a wonderful gift forgiveness is when it covers my failures, mistakes, and sins. I am so thankful for the many years I've lived and walked in God's grace. When I think of how God has forgiven all of my deepest failures and lapses in judgment, I want to tell the world about the power of forgiveness.

But do I want to share actual forgiveness with others?

That is a different story. And I will admit that it is so much easier for me to receive forgiveness than to dispense it to others. Can you relate?

Like many other Christians I know, I struggled for years with the concept and process of forgiving others. At times I was afraid to forgive. My first response was to be self-protective and slow to extend grace. I honestly thought that if I forgave the person who offended me, that same person would gain an advantage over me. Other times, I dug in my heels and held on to my pride and simply did not want to forgive. I didn't feel like the person who hurt me deserved my forgiveness.

On those days when I strived to follow God's example, I would resolve to forgive a person and then some thought of mine or action by them would send me back to a place of hurt and resistance. Believe me, I was never pleased with this inability to forgive. How I hated the obsessive thoughts that accompanied these times of falling short of God's best for me. I despised my own attitudes and irritability. It is a terrible thing to want to do better, to *be* better in an area of obedience to God, and then to witness yourself repeating the same mistakes and misbehaviors over and over.

I remember turning to Matthew 6:14-15 during one such struggle. Jesus's words struck me in a new way as I read: "For if you forgive men their trespasses, your heavenly Father will also forgive you. But if you do not forgive men their trespasses, neither will your Father forgive your trespasses." Honestly, I had always read this like a veiled threat. It had seemed to me as if Jesus was saying, "You'd better forgive others or else!" Suddenly it came to me. Jesus was not threatening me—He was encouraging me. He was saying to me, "Cheryl, if you want to feel the blessed assurance that your own failures, mistakes, and sins are forgiven, *forgive*."

At this juncture, forgiveness took on a whole new look. I realized that forgiveness is something that I do for my own well-being. It is in my best interest to forgive. Before that I believed forgiveness was for the other person's benefit. Forgiveness had felt like a burden rather than a blessing.

From that moment on, I began to choose forgiveness. The choice was not always easy. Sometimes, I had to make that choice again and again in a single conversation. However, some wonderful changes began to take place in my own life as I forgave. I started to experience a new freedom in my walk with Jesus. My friendships with others improved tremendously. I felt God's grace in a palpable way. Not only that, but I was able to grow deeper in my relationship with Jesus.

During the season of growth, I was able to look back with greater clarity on my years of resenting people and actions that offended me. I had held some flat-out wrong perceptions about what forgiveness is and what it entails. The more I explored the Bible and the true meaning of forgiveness, the more empowered I became to release those false concepts.

It's been a few years now of walking in forgiveness. Following through with forgiveness doesn't always come easily, but I am more spiritually prepared to be faithful in this area of life. I can now examine my times of anger, blame, and hurt and look for the sources and triggers. So often there is an underlying issue related to forgiveness. When I choose to forgive, God ratifies that choice and blesses me in the process. Who doesn't want that?

Are you struggling to forgive? Chances are you picked up this book because you're recognizing, like I did, that you aren't experiencing the fullness of God's gift of forgiveness. I don't want in any way to diminish the hurt you feel. No! However, I would love to see you set free from that hurt. I would love for you to be able to have a renewed sense of how much God has already forgiven you. I would love for you to feel the grace of God upon your life in a very real way. I would love for your personal relationship with God to go to a deeper, more intimate, and fulfilling level. I know that all that is possible when, with God's help, you make the choice to forgive.

I invite you to join me on this journey of healing, biblical insight, and true transformation within your heart and, likely, in your relationships. The burden of unforgiveness is too great a weight for you to carry. It is hurting you more than anyone else. It is time for you to be set free!

You are not alone. In the journey ahead, I will share many powerful and encouraging stories of people I know who made the choice to forgive. You will gather hope and strength for your own life's needs as you immerse yourself in stories that could have ended in tragedy, but instead became testimonies of victory all because of one factor—the choice to forgive.

Your victory awaits, my friend.

Chapter 1

God's Great Offer

God has made an amazing offer to mankind—to forgive any man or woman their wrongdoings, sins, and past. God has paid the penalty. Our sins cost the life and death of His only Son. Now, anyone who will accept and believe that Jesus, God's Son, died on the cross for his or her sins will be forgiven by God.

The offer is real and comes with dynamic benefits to all who accept it. The person who receives Jesus also receives all the promises of God that are in Christ Jesus. That means anyone who believes in Jesus can lay claim to a new identity, heaven, God's strength, divine help, and so much more. The Bible describes it like this: "As His divine power has given to us all things that pertain to life and godliness, through the knowledge of Him who called us by glory and virtue, by which have been given to us exceedingly great and precious promises, that through these you may be partakers of the divine nature, having escaped the corruption that is in the world through lust" (2 Peter 1:3-4).

God, in His great compassion and goodness, is extending this offer to you, to me, and to anyone who will simply receive it. It doesn't matter what your past holds or what you have done. God is willing to forgive you if you will allow Him to have the reins of your life.

Have you accepted this great offer? Have you had your sins

forgiven by God? Along with the freedom that comes with forgiving others is understanding the greatness of the forgiveness God is willing to grant to you.

God wants each of us to experience the gift of His forgiveness and the joy of extending grace to others (and to ourselves). The more we explore the fullness of God's grace, the more we'll want to live our lives immersed in it and transformed by it.

Those who accept God's gift discover all He has promised is true!

The Invitation to Transformation

Anna couldn't believe what she was hearing. The pastor at the front of the small church was offering her a brand-new life. He announced that anyone who would walk down to the front of the church and pray would become a new creation and be forgiven of all their past wrongs.

Anna couldn't remember the last time she had been inside a church. Since she was thirteen her life had consisted of drugs, alcohol, and parties. Raised by an alcoholic grandmother in the isolated hills of Santa Inez, Anna had been left mostly alone. She had supported her burgeoning drug addiction by stealing. Over the years she had made promises to try to change to anyone who reached out to her. However, the power of the substances always drew her back into the path of destruction. Friends, family, and well-meaners had given up on the beautiful, petite blonde.

By the time Anna was in her twenties she was living on the streets. One day a friend from high school offered to pay her way to a drug rehabilitation facility. Anna was desperate and accepted his offer.

Anna cooperated fully in the program. She wanted to remain sober, but she feared the cravings that loomed in her soul. While in rehab, she had come to realize the damage and hurt she had inflicted on so many people because of her addiction. The condemnation was overwhelming. When the time for her release came, Anna didn't want to leave.

Throughout the program, her counselors had urged Anna to reach out beyond herself to a higher power to overcome her cravings. Someone had also suggested that she find a church to attend. So the first Sunday after her release, Anna was sitting in the back of the first church she found.

It was in this church that she heard the most beguiling invitation she had ever been offered—a whole new start in life. The pastor said, "Today can be the first day of the rest of your life." That was it! Anna jumped from her seat and rushed down the middle aisle. She wanted that new life. Anna wanted to have her sins and past wiped clean. She wanted to start over with no marks against her. She had no idea if such an offer would ever be given to her again, and she didn't want to miss it.

Anna stood alone at the front only for a moment. The pastor stepped down from the pulpit and put his hand on Anna's shoulder. Soon the whole church gathered around her. They were all crying. The pastor led Anna in a simple prayer asking Jesus to forgive her of all her sins, come and live in her heart, and make her a new creation. From that day forward Anna was a new person.

Today Anna serves in our women's ministry. No one could ever imagine that Anna had such a past. The bright, beautiful blonde with the engaging smile radiates the love and warmth of Jesus. She still tears up when she recalls the invitation that transformed her life.

Anna received a brand-new start in life. You can too. The Bible declares, "If anyone is in Christ, he is a new creation; old things have passed away; behold, all things have become new" (2 Corinthians 5:17). Are you aware of your own need to be forgiven? Do you want a new start? It's only a prayer away.

Too Good to Be True

For some, the offer of God's total forgiveness sounds too incredible. After all, God has promised to wipe away every sin as though it never happened. I had a friend who struggled for some time with this concept. She was frequently haunted at night with memories of the sinful things she had done in her past. One day she prayed, "Lord, if You have wiped out my past and don't remember it anymore, why do I still have such stark reminders?"

Her heart then heard the quiet voice of God speaking: "I have buried your sin in the deepest sea, and I will remember it no more. But I allow you to remember the pain and injury of your sin so that you won't ever return to it."

It's true that God has buried our sins as He promised in Micah 7:18-19, "Who is a God like You, pardoning iniquity and passing over the transgression of the remnant of His heritage? He does not retain His anger forever, because He delights in mercy. He will again have compassion on us, and will subdue our iniquities. You will cast all our sins into the depths of the sea."

Corrie ten Boom used to say that God not only buried our sins in the deepest sea, but He also placed a sign over it saying, "No fishing!"

First John 1:9 promises, "If we confess our sins, He is faithful and just to forgive us our sins and to cleanse us from all unrighteousness." God is faithful to forgive. God will not renege on His offer. He will not fail. What we confess in repentance, He will cancel, wipe out, take out of the way. Not only does God propose to forgive us but to cleanse us as well. God promises to remove the unrighteous origin of the sin that we have confessed.

Think of it like this. Have you ever dealt with mold in your house? Ugh, right? When you deal with mold, it is important to not only clean the places affected by the mold with bleach, but also to get at the source of what is causing the mold. You must deal with the leaky faucet, the dampness, or water problem that produces the mold. Only by taking measures against both the mold and the source of the mold will you effectively deal with the problem. That is what God does when He forgives us. God not only cleans the effects of sin from our lives, but He goes right to the source in our heart that is drawn to the offending behavior.

Jesus dealt with the sin of man on the cross at Calvary. Colossians 2:13-14 describes the accomplishment of Jesus in this way: "And you, being dead in your trespasses and the uncircumcision of your flesh, He has made alive together with Him, having forgiven all your trespasses, having wiped out the handwriting of requirements that was against us, which was contrary to us. And He has taken it out of the way, having nailed it to the cross."

Those who believe in Jesus are forgiven by God of all their trespasses and sins. God sees those past offenses nailed on the cross with Jesus. There is a hymn by Elvina Hall I learned as a child that says, "Jesus paid it all. All to Him I owe. Sin had left a crimson stain, He washed it white as snow." This is exactly what God has done through the death of Jesus on the cross.

Accepting Forgiveness

Mary was getting discouraged. Though she had come to Jesus, her husband Gary did not see his need for forgiveness. Gary was willing to listen to Mary as she shared with him about all the changes that God was bringing into her heart. He even volunteered to listen to the sermon tapes she brought home from church.

For over a year Gary listened to sermons on his way to work and on his commute home. However, Gary seemed totally unmoved by anything he heard. He continued to be emotionally detached from Mary. He drank and partied hard on his boat with his friends every weekend.

Then one morning Gary woke up to the realization that he was a sinner who was well on his way to hell. This realization terrified him. He got in his car to make his commute to work, but was sure he would never make it. Every car seemed to be gunning for him, and Gary was convinced that if he died he would go to hell. Every sin that Gary committed throughout his lifetime, things he never felt bad about before, now served as the prosecuting attorneys against him.

After Gary arrived at work he made a beeline to the telephone in his office. He called the church his wife was attending and made an appointment to see a pastor. He left his office and warily drove to the church, barely surviving the ordeal.

Once at church he spoke to a young pastor there. "I don't want to go to hell and I deserve to go there after all the bad things I have done."

The pastor looked sympathetically at Gary and then opened his Bible to John 3. He explained to Gary that he needed to be born again. Gary agreed, not quite understanding what the pastor meant. The pastor explained to Gary that he could be forgiven by God of every sin he committed if he would ask Jesus to forgive him. Gary nodded. That was exactly what he wanted. Gary wanted God to forgive his sins. Though Gary was only in his early thirties, he wanted the assurance that if he died he would go to heaven. The pastor led Gary in a simple prayer: "Lord Jesus, I admit that I am a sinner. I ask You to forgive me of my sins and come and live in my heart. Amen."

It was so simple, yet Gary felt so free. He left the church and walked out into the bright sunlight of the parking lot feeling a great burden had been rolled off of him. His drive home was exhilarating. The dread was gone.

Until that morning, Gary had never thought of himself as a sinner in need of forgiveness. In fact, he would have scoffed at the term. However, the realization of all the injury that he had caused others hit him that fateful morning. It laid the heavy burden of his own sins upon his shoulders and Gary knew that he was guilty before God. The blessed release had come so easily. He only needed to acknowledge his guilt before God and ask for the accomplishment of Jesus on the cross to be applied to his sin and he was liberated. Gary's life was forever changed.

Admitting You're a Sinner

Most people, like Gary, are unaware of the injury they have

caused to others and their culpability before God. The whole concept of admitting that you are a sinner is really distasteful. However, it is only when we are willing to admit that we owe a debt to God because of our sin that we are ready to want and receive the forgiveness that God offers.

I met Pauline after church on a Sunday morning in London, England. She told me that she was drawn into the church because I smiled at her. Pauline was a beautiful, upper-class woman who just happened to be walking by the school where we held our Sunday morning services.

Pauline asked me who the people gathered at the school were and what we were doing. I explained that we were part of a church that met there. She raised her eyebrows. "My sister is born again. Do you know what that means?"

"Yes, I do." I answered. She asked me to explain it to her. I began by telling her that every person is a sinner according to what the Bible says in Romans 3:23: "For all have sinned and fall short of the glory of God." At this point Pauline laughed. "No, surely not me. I am not a sinner."

Looking at the beautiful woman, I asked the Lord to give me a clear way to clarify this notion to Pauline. "Well, think of it this way. Suppose you parked your car in London so that you could go shopping. Let's say that you were unaware that the spot you chose was not authorized for parking. When you returned to your car you found a great big clamp attached to it and a notice to appear before the magistrate. Then you went down to the council office and were told that you would need to pay a great deal of money to release your car. You told the authorities that you didn't have enough money. Suppose you had a brother…"

At this point Pauline stopped me. "I do have a brother!" she said.

I nodded and continued with my illustration. "All right, then. Your brother finds out that you owe a debt you can't pay so he comes down and pays your debt and frees your car. Now you and your car are free. You don't owe anything to the council but you do owe your brother a great deal. That's the way it is with God. We have done things, many that we are unaware of, that have violated God's rules and ordinances. We do not have the funds or the ability to pay the debt that we owe. So Jesus came and paid the debt we owe to God."

Pauline was thoughtful for a moment. "I see. You are right. I am a sinner then. I want Jesus to pay my debt."

I think that Pauline's problem was a misunderstanding of the term *sinner*. The Greek word used in the New Testament to denote sin is an archery term that literally means, "to miss the mark." In New Testament times when someone was shooting an arrow at a target, unless he hit the dead center of the bull's-eye, he was considered a sinner—he had missed the mark. It didn't matter how far he was from the bull's-eye or how close he came. Any missing of the very center of the target labeled him a sinner.

So when it comes to mankind, God has a certain standard of righteousness. Any missing of that standard of righteousness marks you as a sinner. It doesn't matter if you've committed terrible atrocities or only minor mistakes. You have still missed the mark and need forgiveness for your sin.

Overlooking Our Own Sin

Most of us can more easily recognize the offenses of others than our own. We are very gifted at self-justification and covering and denying our own culpability while pointing the accusatory finger at others. We see our own sins as minor and excusable while others' are major and inexcusable.

That was exactly the way Simon saw it. When we read Luke 7:36-50 we discover that Simon had invited Jesus into his house for a meal. Though the common courtesy of Simon's day was to wash your guest's feet, anoint them with the signature oil of the house, and greet your guests with a kiss, Simon had not shown any of these courtesies to Jesus. Rather, Simon had virtually ignored Jesus. We are not told whether Simon omitted the basic courtesies purposely or he simply forgot.

A woman of bad reputation arrived while Jesus was in Simon's house. This woman immediately made her way to Jesus. She fell down before Him and poured oil from an alabaster flask onto His feet. Then she began to wash His feet with her tears and wipe them with her hair.

Simon was disgusted at this display and reasoned in his heart, "This Man (Jesus), if He were a prophet, would know who and what manner of woman this is who is touching Him, for she is a sinner."

Jesus, knowing what was going through Simon's mind, said, "Simon, I have something to say to you."

Simon replied, "Teacher, say it."

Jesus shared a parable with Simon. The parable had to do with two men who owed a great debt. The first man owed thousands of dollars while the other man owed only a few. The creditor agreed to cancel both men's debts. "Tell Me, therefore, which of them will love him more?"

Simon replied, "I suppose the one whom he forgave more."

Jesus then looked at the woman. "Do you see this woman? I entered your house; you gave Me no water for My feet, but she has washed My feet with her tears and wiped them with the hair of her head. You gave Me no kiss, but this woman has not ceased to kiss My feet since the time I came in. You did not anoint My head with oil, but this woman has anointed My feet with fragrant oil. Therefore I say to you, her sins, which are many, are forgiven, for she loved much. But to whom little is forgiven, the same loves little."

The woman was conscious of her own sinful condition. She knew she had missed the mark and needed forgiveness. In acknowledging her sin and need of Jesus, the woman had received the divine forgiveness of Christ. The woman, because of her love and gratitude for Jesus, had afforded Him all the courtesies that Simon had neglected. She had washed Jesus's feet. She had anointed them with fragrant oil. She had kissed His feet again and again.

Simon had missed the mark. Priding himself in his own righteousness, he had neglected to show due diligence to Jesus. His neglect was sinful and placed him in the same category as the woman with the bad reputation.

All Have Sinned

Isaiah 53:6 proclaims, "All we like sheep have gone astray; we have turned, every one, to his own way; and the LORD has laid on Him the iniquity of us all." There is not one person living on the earth who has not sinned. Every person has missed the mark that God requires. Every man and woman has gone astray and turned to his or her own way. God has allowed Jesus to pay the penalty for those sins that we have committed. Now to receive that glorious forgiveness of sin God offers we only need to admit that we have indeed sinned and need the atoning death of Jesus to pay the penalty we have incurred.

The process of acceptance of forgiveness by God is so simple. We need only pray, acknowledging that we have sinned, and ask God to forgive us for our sins because of what Jesus has done on the cross.

God wants to forgive your sins. God wants you to experience the wondrous sense of emancipation that comes from God cancelling your sins and burying them in the deepest sea. The Psalmist describes it this way in Psalm 103:11-12, "For as the heavens are high above the earth, so great is His mercy toward those who fear Him; as far as the east is from the west, so far has He removed our transgressions from us."

Questions for Study and Personal Reflection

1. Read Luke 7:36-50. What ministers to you most about this story?

2. Who do you relate to most—Simon or the woman who was a known sinner?

3. What sins do you need to acknowledge before God?

4. How will you claim 1 John 1:9 over those sins you just acknowledged?

5. Use Isaiah 53:4-6 to briefly explain how Jesus paid the penalty for your sin.

6. Examine Micah 7:19: "He will again have compassion on us, and will subdue our iniquities. You will cast all our sins into the depths of the sea." List any sins that you need to reckon as being "cast into the depths of the sea" by God. Remember, "No fishing!"

Prayer

Dear Lord,

You so readily cover me with Your grace. You take my sins and cast them into the sea where I cannot retrieve them and try to hold on to them once again. Today, I ask for forgiveness of all of my sins.

I accept the invitation to be transformed by Your forgiveness. I long to fully understand and embrace my identity as a saved child of God.

Give me a heart that is willing and eager to extend forgiveness to others. Each time I hand one of my sins over to Your grace, remind me that there is someone in my life who also needs to experience this great gift. In Jesus's name, amen.

Chapter 2

The True Meaning of Forgiveness

For many years my struggle with forgiveness revolved around my misconceptions about what forgiveness meant and entailed. These false beliefs kept me from being willing to open up the door to forgiveness, fearful that even greater injury would come.

Have you stumbled over the same fear? Or maybe there is a different false view of forgiveness which keeps your heart frozen and unwilling to forgive. Misconceptions about forgiveness are dangerous. They not only keep us from enjoying freedom we are intended to experience, but they interfere with the process of forgiveness. For many people I know, those misunderstandings have become barriers. Like me, the moment they started believing the misconceptions rather than truth, they became stuck. It is when we discern and then discard lies that we become able to receive forgiveness and enabled to forgive others.

As we explore some of these misconceptions, we'll uncover how they are false, how we can let go of them, and how we can move toward giving and receiving forgiveness.

Misconception One: Forgiveness Means "Whatever It Takes"

Not too long after Brian and I were married, I began to have struggles with a young woman I was spending time with. She was constantly competing with me. I hated it. When we shopped together she would point to the ugliest outfit in the vicinity and say, "Oh, that looks just like you." Then she would point to an adorable outfit and add, "And that one looks just like me."

There were other comparisons that made life simply miserable. The tension all came to a head after our children were born. It was one thing to put me down, but don't touch my baby! There was a falling out between us and I withdrew completely from the friendship. I felt she had crossed the line and I wasn't ready to let her return back into my life. Instinctively I wanted to protect my baby daughter.

Then one day I heard a pastor preaching on forgiveness on the radio. My conscience was pricked. This woman's name immediately came to mind. I knew I needed to make it right. The pastor said that I needed to do "whatever it took" to have the relationship restored. Ugh…the past relationship had been so unhealthy. Nevertheless, if that was what God was requiring, then that was what I would have to do. I needed to do "whatever it took" to restore the relationship.

I made a call to the woman and apologized for my part in the failed friendship. She asked if we could get together with our husbands and renew the social interaction. I said yes, and we agreed to go to dinner.

I was hopeful about the restoration and willing to do "whatever it took," but I soon realized that it was impossible. Brian and I picked the couple up in our car and we all headed out to dinner. It wasn't long before the insults began to fly at me from the backseat. I held my peace; after all, I had agreed to do "whatever it took." The evening was miserable. I took the blame for everything that had gone wrong in the friendship as well as some extra blame for other things that had gone wrong in her life. It was grueling.

Arriving home, Brian said to me, "I don't think you should try so hard to renew that relationship. I don't think it's healthy."

I explained to him what I had heard the preacher say on the radio and how I wanted to truly forgive from my heart.

It was then that Brian explained to me the true meaning of forgiveness. Forgiveness was not doing "whatever it took" to restore a relationship. Forgiveness meant to "cancel a debt." Therefore, forgiveness did not require that I go back under the duress of insults and comparisons, but rather that I simply cancel the debt I felt owed to me because of what I had endured.

I could forgive and reinstate a friendship with healthy boundaries. The whole notion of "whatever it took" was not a healthy proposition. It did not benefit my friend or myself to have a relationship without mutual respect for each other.

Is it any wonder that people are afraid to forgive? To forgive under the pretext of doing whatever it takes is dangerous at best. It leaves the one who forgives vulnerable to more and even greater injury.

Forgiveness is a state of the heart and does not require that emotional or physical boundaries be removed and a relationship be reinstated.

Misconception Two: Forgiveness Is Pretending It Never Happened

God delights in truth. God never requires that we live in the area of fantasy, blocking out or denying the wrong that was done to us. In fact, God wants us to see the full brunt of the damage that has been inflicted and then cancel the debt. He never asks us to pretend an offense didn't occur or have an effect on us.

Recently, a friend was talking about the unscrupulous behavior of someone I knew. Someone else cautioned, "But you must forgive them."

I knew my friend had already forgiven that person from the heart. It is not unforgiving to assess the full amount of injury so that the full debt can be cancelled. Denial of any injury or downplaying the injury only leads to false thinking.

It was just a few weeks before Christmas. My dad, Chuck Smith, was recovering from back surgery, and I was sitting in his hospital room. I heard the familiar ping on my telephone that told me I had gotten a text message. I opened up the text to see a picture of the totally crashed-in front grill of my daughter's Honda. The caption underneath simply said, "Oops."

You can imagine my dismay. It was so close to Christmas, and our finances were already tight. My daughter was in school and had no resources to pay for the damages. The accident was totally her fault. She hadn't seen the brake lights on the truck in front of her in time.

My husband took the car to our good friend, Abe. It was beneficial for us to know the details of the damage done. To ignore any of the mechanical troubles would've compromised our daughter's safety and eventually been more costly. Abe told us the extent of the damage and gave us the estimate for a complete restoration. We paid the debt in full.

Acknowledging the full impact of our heart and life injuries allows us to forgive the whole offense. How many times have you forgiven someone only to find that the damage done was worse than you realized? I don't know about you, but when this has happened to me, I find that I have to go back to the drawing board and ask God to help me to forgive all over again.

Misconception Three: Forgiving Is Forgetting

Some people have an amazing ability to forget that wrong was ever done to them. Other people think they are unable to forgive simply because they can remember the offending incident that happened.

Forgetting does not always accompany forgiveness. God promises in Hebrews 8:12, "For I will be merciful to their unrighteousness, and their sins and their lawless deeds I will remember no more." This "remembering no more" is not forgetting, but refusing to bring them as charges against us. In other words, God is promising to drop the charges against us. Like a judge who rules the evidence against the defendant as inadmissible, so God rules our sins as being inadmissible. They cannot be used against us in any way. They have been forgiven. The sins are covered and paid for.

Patty was overjoyed to hear that her brother had accepted the Lord. Yet she still held some reservations about him. She could still clearly remember the unholy groping of her body and the robbery of her innocence. She didn't want her own children around her brother. Did that mean she still held a grudge against her brother for his violation of her when they were younger?

Was she refusing to extend to him the forgiveness God so fully granted him?

Patty prayed. One day she felt compelled to call her brother. She began the conversation with small talk about their mom, dad, and mutual friends. Midway during the conversation Patty blurted out, "I forgive you for robbing me of my innocence. I forgive you for molesting me when I was a child." There was silence for a moment on the other end of the line. Patty waited, her hands shaking as she held the receiver to her ears. Then she heard it—the muffled sound of crying. Her brother was weeping.

"I am so sorry," he cried. "Thank you for forgiving me."

In that moment Patty felt a great weight lifted. She had not forgotten the offense, nor would she ever, but it no longer held the power over her that it once did. It no longer defined who she was or what she became. She was free.

Misconception Four: Forgiving Someone Requires Letting Them Back into Our Lives

Jesus as our Good Shepherd desires to protect us. When I was a child, I never left the house without hearing my mother's admonition, "Remember, you are a lamb among wolves." This was my mom's way of warning me that some people out in the world weren't trustworthy. The best way to keep from being eaten by a wolf is to recognize and avoid him.

Jane kept forgiving her brother-in-law. Nevertheless, he made life miserable for her. He was constantly causing trouble in her marriage. He would call daily and insist on having lengthy conversations with his brother, Jane's husband. During the course of these conversations, Jim would malign Jane. She sensed a mildly distant attitude from her husband after every phone call. These disturbances, in combination with her brother-in-law's drug addiction and frequent need to be bailed out of bad situations, took an emotional and physical toll on Jane. She wanted to forgive Jim, but she was afraid that would require letting Jim dominate her marriage and husband. So Jane refused to forgive.

The more Jane continued to let the unforgiveness toward her brother-in-law fester, the more she felt herself turning into the shrew that Jim accused her of being. Yet, for Jane, the stakes of forgiving were much too high. She couldn't risk it.

Her marriage began to suffer. She found herself not only hostile to her brother-in-law, but now the hostility transferred onto her husband as well. They sought out their pastor's advice.

The pastor listened as Jane and her husband poured out their mutual grievances toward each other. Then the pastor looked at Jane and said, "You need to forgive your husband." At this point Jane began to cry.

"I can't," she said. Then she admitted, "I'm afraid to."

"What is it you are afraid of?" the pastor probed. Jane laid out a myriad of fears, beginning with losing all their money to the brother-in-law and culminating in the loss of her marriage if she chose to forgive her husband.

"Why do you think this will happen if you forgive him?"

"If I forgive him he won't be accountable to me. He will let his brother dominate our marriage."

The pastor explained to Jane that her own inability to forgive her husband was causing the alienation of affection and actually putting the brother-in-law in closer proximity. "Forgiveness does not mean that you allow your husband to let your brother-in-law take all your money or sow discord between the two of you. It simply means that you don't hold your husband accountable for your brother-in-law's actions. Your husband is not your brother-in-law."

Jane prayed with the pastor and her husband for the power to forgive. The Lord granted her that power that very hour. She came to realize that when she forgave her husband, she actually removed her brother-in-law from their marriage.

Soon after this release, Jane's husband took the initiative to distance himself from his brother. Without Jane's prodding, her husband saw the injury his own brother was doing to his marriage and livelihood. For Jane and her husband, forgiveness meant keeping the brother-in-law from being so closely involved in their lives.

Misconception Five: You Must Go to the Offender in Order to Forgive

For some people the idea of having to be in the same room as the one who injured them is terrifying. Those who consider confrontation as a necessary aspect of forgiveness often put off forgiving until they feel confident enough to face their offender. It is not necessary to have a face-to-face confrontation with the person who hurt or offended you.

I have often heard people use Matthew 18:15-17 to insist on an in-person confrontation. However, those who do so are taking Jesus's admonition out of context. "Moreover if your brother sins against you, go and tell him his fault between you and him alone. If he hears you, you have gained your brother. But if he will not hear, take with you one or two more, that 'by the mouth of two or three witnesses every word may be established.' And if he refuses to hear them, tell it to the church. But if he refuses even to hear the church, let him be to you like a heathen and a tax collector."

This passage of Scripture has to do with the restoration of a sister or brother to the church. Restoration requires repentance. This passage does not have to do with whether or not you are to forgive someone. Neither is this passage dealing with the means by which you forgive someone.

Forgiveness begins as a private transaction between you and God that takes place in the heart. After forgiveness is worked out in the heart with God, it then manifests outwardly in a myriad of unique and different ways.

Some people are never safe. Every word you say to them can and will be held against you. Does this mean they are excluded from forgiveness? No, not at all. It simply means that the act of forgiveness does not require their presence. The account is settled in your heart with God.

When Jesus spoke of forgiving in Matthew 18:35, He spoke of a transaction in the heart. "So My heavenly Father also will do to you if each of you, from his heart, does not forgive his brother his trespasses."

There are some people who will only trample on the tenderness extended to them in forgiveness. This, at times, can be counterproductive to the process of forgiving. Remember that forgiveness is an activity of the heart that is first between you and God alone.

Misconception Six: Forgiveness Changes the Person Who Is Forgiven

When Tina forgave her mother for years of verbal abuse and neglect, she expected to see some sign of change in her mom. She started to wonder if she had not forgiven correctly. One night as Tina was praying, she felt an urgency in her spirit to forgive her mother again. Each wrong her mother had committed replayed in her mind, and Tina forgave one after another. The experience was exhilarating. Tina was sure this experience would have a positive impact on her relationship with her mother.

Tina called her mom and asked if she could come for a visit. Tina's mom was apprehensive, but Tina was so excited about her new attitude, she soon convinced her mom it was a good idea. So she flew out to see the woman she had forgiven.

The visit started out well. The women embraced and Tina's mom seemed to love having her daughter there. However, after only two days, Tina's mom began to drink again. As the drinking increased so did her mother's verbal attacks. "Why did you come here?" her mother challenged her in a menacing voice. "I was always so disappointed in you. You've always been a loser." The cruelty continued to escalate to the point where Tina called her brother and asked him to come and rescue her from her mother's attacks.

While Tina waited in the guest room, she could hear her mother screaming insults from the living room. Tina fell to her knees. "God, I chose to forgive her. So what went wrong?"

"Nothing," was the simple answer Tina heard deep within her heart. "This is the person you forgave. This is the person you must continue to forgive."

Tina picked up the phone and dialed her brother. "I'm going to stay," she said.

Something in Tina had changed. Where resentment and hurt once dominated in Tina's heart, pity and love overflowed. She watched for ways to help the woman she was forgiving. When she noticed her mom walking as though in pain, Tina grabbed moisturizer and began to massage her feet. "Mom, I know your life was not easy," she said. "You made some mistakes. But you raised Ted and me. You always made sure we were fed and had a roof over our heads. I want to thank you for that."

The visit ended like it had begun, with the two women embracing. Tina's mother continued to viciously attack her during intermittent phone calls, but the abuse seemed to lose its sting after a time. Her mother did not change. The relationship never developed into the relationship Tina longed for. However, Tina changed. She was able to forgive her mom for being an alcoholic and a verbally abusive person. The forgiveness that Tina showed to her mother did have dividends.

When Tina's mom was sober and dying in the hospital she requested that Tina come to her bedside. There in the sterile hospital room, Tina was able to lead her mom to Jesus before she died. Tina confided in me that though she and her mom had a bad relationship on earth, she is confident that once in heaven, they will have a better relationship than she could ever imagine.

Misconception Seven: Forgiveness Rehearses Details

It is not necessary to rehearse and dredge up every infraction and every wrong done in order to forgive someone. At times forgiveness will require choosing a blanket pardon to cover the entire past history you share with a person.

In Philippians 3:13, the apostle Paul wrote, "Brethren, I do not count myself to have apprehended; but one thing I do, forgetting those things which are behind and reaching forward to those things which are ahead." There are times when forgiveness will mean choosing not to dig up every past offense. It will mean laying it all to rest in one fell swoop.

Misconception Eight: Forgiveness Is Gained by Paying Our Own Debt

A problem often arises when we try to atone or pay for our own forgiveness. When this becomes our view of how grace works, we also expect others to pay for their own debt. Whether you are trying to earn forgiveness or you are challenging others to earn their own, you encounter a path of lies and struggles.

We try to earn God's forgiveness by doing as many good works as possible or by berating ourselves incessantly for messing up. Have you been guilty of this? I know I have.

I remember really messing up a few years ago. Some people sin privately. It seems that I have the propensity to do it publicly. Ugh.

It happened on a Friday morning when I was teaching for my mom. The subject was love. What a great topic, right? In the course of teaching I happened to mention a certain actor and I said, "I really hate him." I could hear the gasp in the audience. I suddenly realized how contradictory my statement was to all those to whom I was trying to communicate. It got worse! I tried to cover my indiscretion by elaborating on some of the bad things this actor had done. I was burying myself alive in the hole that I had dug. Finally, I just stopped. I apologized to the women and had them pray with me for this actor.

I felt terrible for weeks after that. I apologized to any woman I met who had attended the study. When my mom, who had been in Israel at the time, arrived home, I went immediately to her house. I explained what I had done and then begged for her forgiveness. I even volunteered never to teach another study again if that would help.

I have to admit my mom was taken aback with what I had done. "Oh, dear me" was her first response. Then she said, "Cheryl, we all sin and do stupid things. That's why we need Jesus. I think you just showed those women a living example of how desperately we need Him."

One day I was elaborating on the whole ordeal to a young man who wasn't even present at the study and hadn't heard about my blunder. Suddenly he stopped me in the middle of my story. "Cheryl, why are you telling me this? I wasn't even there. Are you trying to atone for your sin by confessing it to as many people as possible?"

I looked at him in amazement. That was exactly what I was trying to do. I was trying to earn God's forgiveness by letting everyone know how stupid I had been. I went home and sought the Lord alone in my room. God began to speak to my heart. "Cheryl, if you discovered an ugly, dirty, corroded shoe in your closet, what would you do with it?"

"I would throw it away immediately and clean out my closet," I answered.

The Lord spoke to me again, "Would you tell everyone about the shoe? Would you display it in your house as a sign to everyone about the ugliness that came out of your closet?"

Of course the answer was no. I would simply get rid of the offending object, clean my closet, and make sure that didn't happen again. The Lord ministered to me that this was exactly what He wanted me to do with my sin.

The way to deal with it was simply to ask God's forgiveness, claiming what He already promised to me because of Jesus, and move on. Oh, but it seemed so simple. It took the responsibility off of me and put it all on Jesus.

A sense of thanksgiving and appreciation flooded my soul. I began to praise and thank Jesus for His wondrous forgiveness. I found myself singing the words to the old hymn "He Paid a Debt He Did Not Owe" by Ellis J. Crum. Such songs remind me that I have debts I could never, ever repay and that only God can wash those away from my life.

That day I realized the substantial forgiving power of God. It was greater than the debt I owed. It was generously applied to my liability. It washed the sin away.

I learned that I could not atone for my sin in any way. It was God who showed me the offense, and it was God who freely forgave that same offense and cleansed me of the unrighteousness within.

Learning to forgive others must begin with the acknowledgment that God has forgiven us for every wrong we have committed. That is the same forgiveness we are to extend to others.

Are you trying to atone for your own sins? Are you berating yourself and telling yourself you are worthless because of those sins? Dear sister, simply confess them to Jesus and be free of them by faith. Receiving the forgiveness of Jesus is an act of faith. You must believe that your sins are forgiven on the basis of what He has done on the cross and promised in His Word. You are not forgiven because you deserve to be forgiven or on the merit of good works you have done or even because you feel ashamed of the things you have done. No! You are forgiven because the blood of Jesus Christ is so powerful that it alone will forgive and cleanse you from every sin you have committed or will ever commit.

Today you are loved and forgiven because you have acknowledged your sin before God and asked Him to forgive you because of Jesus. Remember, God in His faithfulness is perfectly just to forgive you all your sins and cleanse you from all unrighteousness!

These misconceptions have turned many people away from embracing forgiveness. So if forgiving doesn't mean doing whatever it takes, pretending it never happened, forgetting the offense, letting the offender back into one's life, facing the offender, or expecting a change in the offender or circumstances, what does it mean?

What Forgiveness Is

The simplest definition of forgiveness is the cancelling of a debt.

The term used in the New Testament concerning forgiveness is an accounting term. It has to do with something owed to another person. Sin and offense takes something from us. Offenses include stealing our innocence, violating our trust, diminishing our character by insult or slander, robbing us of a possession, destroying a relationship, ruining our sense of well-being, inflicting physical injury, and damaging property. In the Law of Moses, when something was taken, violated, injured, or destroyed, restitution was always required. That restitution was a lien against the one who had done the injury. Until the lien was paid, the one who incurred the damage was indebted to the one to whom they caused the damage.

In the Lord's Prayer, Jesus uses the words "debts" and "debtors" in reference to forgiveness. He instructs to pray in this manner: "forgive us our debts, as we forgive our debtors."

Perhaps you've incurred a financial debt. Maybe you made

payments on a car, washing machine, or credit card. You are a debtor to the company until you've made the final payment. When the last payment is made, you are *forgiven*. You are no longer a debtor.

Let's take it a step further and say you were unable to make the payments, neglected the payments, missed the payments, or refused to pay them. Whether or not you intentionally missed your payment doesn't matter to those who are owed. You are a debtor until every payment is made.

Now let's say someone stepped in—a friend or a nice person—and paid all you owed. Then you would owe that person rather than the company. You are no longer a debtor to the company, but you have become a debtor to your benefactor.

Jesus is our benefactor. He has paid the debts we owed because of sin.

Consider how amazing it is that God forgives our debt no matter how huge it is. There isn't anything you can do or imagine doing that God's grace would not cover. If you are a woman who still has a hard time believing this, pay special attention to every story I share in this book. You will be in awe of the extent, depth, and beauty of God's forgiveness.

Unforgiveness Takes Up Room in Our Hearts

Sitting one morning in front of a cozy fireplace reading my Bible, the Lord gave me a vision. In my mind I saw my heart as a treasure cave. There were many beautiful objects inside this cave. But my line of sight came across a huge black cast-iron safe. I focused my attention on the safe and was startled when it opened to reveal torn and tattered papers inside. I pulled one out to inspect it. The papers had bite marks all along the perimeter as though a rodent had chewed on them. There were soiled spots all over the documents.

"These are what you have been keeping in the recesses of your heart," I heard a voice say.

"What are they?" I asked, not recognizing the papers.

"They are the liens you are holding against others for the injuries they have inflicted upon you."

As I examined the papers in the vision, I realized they were indictments against others I had drawn up in my own heart.

The one that I was first given to examine was against a young man I had overheard talking against me. My mind flashed back to the time of the incident. Brian and I had extended hospitality and our home to this man, Tom, during a time when we also were hosting a young couple. It was a full house but we were glad to open our lives up to each person.

One day, as I was putting away the clean clothes I had just folded, I heard my name mentioned in conversation from the next room. I stopped what I was doing, unsure if someone was trying to speak to me. But nobody was trying to get my attention. Instead, I was hearing Tom talk about me to the couple. "I don't like Cheryl," he said. "I think Brian could have done a lot better than Cheryl."

I was shocked! This young man was staying in my house, eating and enjoying the food I was making. He was using the towels and bedding I was providing for him.

At that moment I didn't know whether I should continue to listen or walk away. I chose to walk away, but the pain of the offense lingered. The young man continued to be in our lives for years to follow. He would call Brian at various times and to say that I resented his phone calls is an understatement. He would keep Brian on the phone for hours arguing about this or that. Another time I overheard him insulting my father and contradicting a message he had just given.

Every time this man's name was mentioned I seethed inside. Whenever I had a private moment with Brian, I would bring out the charges I held against him and rehearse them again and again.

Now, years later, in the vision of the treasure cave, I am asked to examine the tattered paper representing the indictment I held in my heart against Tom. I realize it is crumpled from the many times I took it out of the treasury of my heart and then quickly shoved it back in.

"God, what is it You want me to do with these indictments?" I asked.

"I want you to give them to Me."

In that moment God was asking for every lien that I had ever held against anyone in my life. What I had considered as something worthy of carrying around in my heart—an accusation that demanded payment from the one who had caused the injury—now looked like trash. Not only did it take up room in my heart, it polluted my heart.

One by one, I gave the liens I held against others to God. If there was any debt to be extracted, it was God's to extract, not mine. I cancelled the debt I felt others owed me by giving all the debts to God.

What do you carry in your heart today that once seemed important to keep but now feels like a soiled piece of litter?

Let's review a list of what forgiveness isn't and what it is. Take time with each of these truths and let them sink in. Take a few moments to ask yourself if you have let misconceptions rule your attitude toward another person or toward the act of forgiveness.

- It is not doing whatever it takes to restore a relationship.
- It is not pretending an offense never happened.
- It is not the ability to completely forget the past.
- It is not necessarily confronting the offender.
- It is not a promise that the offender will change.
- It is not a means to change the offender or the offense.
- It is not rehearsing, reliving, and rehashing every wrong done against you.
- It *is* giving all your grievances against others to God.

- It *is* cancelling the debt others owe to you.

- It *is* giving all you owe and are owed to God.

- It *is* a great gift from God that has no limit.

Misconceptions about forgiveness can keep the most sincere people from forgiving. However, when you realize forgiveness is an act of the heart between you and God which results in the cancellation of debt owed, it is no longer frightening but beautiful. The time has come to be willing to cancel the debts you've held against others that you might be free to fill the treasury of your heart with all the good things God desires to put into it.

The process of forgiveness is not frightening but freeing. Are you ready to start?

Questions for Study and Personal Reflection

1. List any misconceptions you have had about forgiveness.

2. Read Matthew 18:21-35. How is forgiveness manifested in this story?

3. What warning does this Scripture present for those who refuse to forgive?

4. List any fears or apprehensions you have held onto about forgiving others.

5. Why do you desire to choose to forgive now? What is your hope as you walk in this journey?

Prayer

Dear God,

I reflect now on the times I have embraced misconceptions about forgiveness instead of turning to Your truth. Free me from false understandings today so I can stand on Your promises for me and my life. Give me a hunger for Your Word, Your guidance, and Your compassion.

When I'm afraid that forgiveness negates the pain I experienced or the other person's role in that pain, release me from that concern. Thank You for the freedom of forgiveness. It has set me free from the confinement of fear. In Jesus's name, amen.

Chapter 3

Why We Hold Back

Sometimes we discover that we are reluctant to forgive. We hold back from embracing grace or we hold on to unforgiveness. Funny enough, the word "unforgiveness" doesn't actually exist. You can't find it in Webster's. However, the symptoms and consequences withholding forgiveness *can* be found. Most of us don't have to look much further than our own lives for examples of how being unforgiving wounds us and others. For the sake of being able to identify the resentment that lingers in our hearts when we haven't forgiven, we will employ the non-existent word and deem it legitimate for the purpose of exploration and understanding.

While we are at it, let's define this word. I consider unforgiveness to be the holding of grudges in the heart against someone. It is the state of being unable to pardon another for what they have done or continue to do. Unforgiveness is evidenced by feelings of resentment, anger, and hostility toward an individual.

In the last chapter we discussed some of the misconceptions about forgiveness so we could clearly see what it truly is—the cancelling of a debt. In this chapter we'll discuss the origins of unforgiveness in order to understand its strength and hold on the human heart.

How Unforgiveness Takes Root

Resentment. It was there before Sally even knew she was dealing with it. She was constantly upset with Joan. In fact, her primary topic of conversation *became* Joan, not because she liked Joan, but just the opposite: Joan bothered her. Joan made her feel like she was a naughty child. Joan was always critiquing her work and showing Sally where she came up short. Joan used a condescending voice, words, and gestures whenever she talked to Sally. Furthermore, Joan always addressed Sally publicly, letting everyone in the office know how Sally had messed up.

Joan, Joan, Joan. Every night Sally's family was treated to another account of what Joan had said or done. Soon Sally had a whole list of Joan's offenses locked up tight in her heart. They were written in novel form, and at any given moment, Joan could pull out a chapter and retell the story of what Joan had done in vivid detail.

Sally had no idea she was struggling with unforgiveness. She really believed she was just making observations about Joan and her problems. Joan was untrustworthy, mean-spirited, and critical. Joan also had an agenda, or so Sally had come to believe.

One day, as Sally was having lunch with a friend, she plunged into the latest installment in the Joan saga. The look on her friend's face told her that she was not enjoying this newest chapter. Her friend looked more and more uncomfortable as Sally added emotional fervor to her story.

The friend interrupted her mid-sentence. "Sally, you need to forgive Joan."

Sally was dumbfounded. "I don't have anything against Joan. Joan has the problems."

Her friend looked sympathetically at Sally. "As your friend, I am telling you that this thing with Joan is beginning to take over your life. In the beginning you were just bothered by her, but now you are preoccupied by her. Joan's name comes up in every conversation we have."

Sally realized her friend was right. How had things gone this far? When had her grievances with Joan imbedded themselves into the lining of her heart? What had caused the resentment to bury itself so deeply? She had no idea when the grievances against Joan had taken root and turned lethal. She tried to remember when or what incident caused it to suddenly catch in her heart. She had so many causes against Joan it was hard to choose just one. Then she realized it came when she decided to start keeping score.

Like Sally, some people don't detect when or how unforgiveness slowly enters the heart and takes root. It is only after the symptoms begin to manifest themselves—symptoms like preoccupation with the offender—that you realize unforgiveness has taken root in your heart.

Injury

There are many different causes for unforgiveness. Some causes are obvious and strong. I recently watched a movie called *Heaven's Rain*. It is the true story of a young man who struggled to forgive the men who brutally murdered his parents, raped his sister, and stole his parents' wedding rings and valuables. The character's anger and unforgiveness toward his parents' murderers is totally understandable. What is remarkable about his story is how he forgave the murderers.

Other injuries are not so serious. Julie struggled all throughout high school to forgive the girl who stole her boyfriend in ninth grade. Even after Julie was happily married with two children, she struggled to release the feelings of anger and resentment she had held so long.

Unforgiveness does not require a dramatic scenario. In fact, the causes can range from petty to tremendous. Once a person begins to hold unforgiveness in an area or against a person, it soon spreads throughout the heart. As it strengthens its case against the first offense, unforgiveness soon finds more causes against others. It's like a lawyer who gathers witnesses for his court case and keeps adding one offense after another against the plaintiff.

The first cause does not always take root. Sometimes it is the secondary causes that make the offense grow into the festering weed of unforgiveness.

Frustration

Dee is the only believer in her family and has been since she accepted the Lord in 1976. For Dee it is a daily struggle to deal with her husband, as well as the three other adult family members who live in her home. These other members hold different values and priorities than Dee. They are easily offended and band together often against her. Any attempt to confront the problems only leads to the issue being twisted around until Dee is made out to be unreasonable. More than once she has found herself angry, resentful, and frustrated.

Dee hadn't realized how her mounting frustrations were turning into a cauldron of unforgiveness until Christmastime last year. Even though she was the only employed member of the household, working a steady job that required 40 hours a week, it was incumbent upon her to provide and prepare the family's favorite Christmas morning brunch. The dishes the family expected were complicated and time-consuming, ranging from appetizers to desserts.

By the time Christmas morning arrived, Dee was exhausted. Unwilling to have another incident at Christmastime, Dee continued to serve the adult members of the household. While they sat on the couch, watched television, and indulged in video games, Dee set the table, served the food, washed the dishes, and straightened the house. Dee soon realized that, as usual, she had been abandoned to the duties of Christmas alone. No one volunteered or even lifted one finger to help. They didn't even acknowledge how hard she worked to put Christmas on for them. There was no sense of gratitude at all. The mounting resentment soon manifested itself. Dee was through!

Dee announced her resignation and retreated into her bedroom. It was the only place where she could enjoy some semblance of privacy in the overly crowded house.

No sooner had Dee closed the door than she felt the conviction of the Lord. The Lord showed Dee that her unforgiveness was manifested in her rotten attitude. Dee had to sort through and itemize the things she was angry about and where she had failed. Once she did she gave the whole thing to the Lord. Immediately, she felt the release that comes from giving all your frustrations to God.

That day the Lord showed her that sin creates a true debt but Christ's blood paid for each and every one of those debts. Just as she could not continue to require a payment from a financial debt that had already been paid, so she felt that she could not hold a spiritual debt against another because Jesus had already paid their debt.

Once she recognized that she was dealing with unforgiveness she was able to apply the payment of Jesus's blood against their offense. Dee has found this practice to be a great weapon against unforgiveness.

Unfortunately, the members of Dee's family have not changed in their behavior toward Dee. Situations like the one at Christmas continue to develop, but Dee has learned to recognize and deal with unforgiveness at its first inception.

Retribution

There is some deep longing in each of us for retribution. We want justice. We want to see the bad guys get what is coming to them. We want the evildoer to be punished. However, the desire for retribution, if given enough nurturing, can turn into a dangerous form of unforgiveness that demands vengeance.

Years ago I was sewing a quilt in the room next to our family room. Through the open door I could hear bad language and violent sounds coming from our television set. I marched into the family room with every bit of righteous indignation resident in me and turned off the offending video. My husband, who was sitting on the couch with my son, was outraged. "What have you done?" he cried. "The bad guys were just about to get it!"

"Brian, there was so much bad language and violence coming from it. I don't want our son exposed to that."

Brian was still unconvinced. "But the bad guys were just about to get it," he repeated.

"Brian, if some people came to our door talking like that, would you let them into our house?"

The answer was obvious. Brian ordinarily would have refused to let the scenes and language that were taking place on the screen be seen or heard in our house. However, he had gotten hooked by his desire to see just retribution meted out to the bad guys.

What is it within us that craves justice? I believe it is the residue of our Maker still resident in every person He created.

But vengeance is dangerous. It takes retribution a step beyond justice. The Law of Moses was not demanding justice but putting a limitation on the thirst for vengeance in man. "But if any harm follows, then you shall give life for life, eye for eye, tooth for tooth, hand for hand, foot for foot, burn for burn, wound for wound, stripe for stripe" (Exodus 21:23-25).

When we are hurt or injured we want to strike back and do greater harm to the person that hurt us than what was done to us. If you cheat me out of a dollar I want at least two dollars in return for the pain and suffering of being cheated out of the one!

I have two grandsons who often wrestle. Just the other day as the older grandson passed by his little brother he mussed up his hair. His little brother was angry and right away went for his brother's coiffured hair. The little brother didn't want to just tousle his hair; he wanted to pull it out by the roots!

That's how the unforgiveness manifested itself in my friend Heidi. She had married at age 19 and moved in with her in-laws so she and her husband could finish college. It seemed like a good arrangement; however, Heidi quickly realized that her father-in-law, Bob, was not caring and supportive like her father. The tone in her husband's home was very different.

Bob was an extremely self-absorbed, coldhearted, manipulative, and belligerent man. He constantly criticized and berated his wife. Even so, Heidi's mother-in law, Dina, treated her husband with the utmost respect and care. She worked hard all week in order to provide her family with necessities and simple extras that her husband refused to give them.

Heidi became outraged as she witnessed Bob's abuse and controlling behavior. When she tried to stick up for her mother-in-law, her efforts were either ignored or thwarted. Soon, her thoughts became filled with ways to get even with Bob for his cruelty. She even fantasized about ways to murder him. These thoughts brought her a sense of comfort and control.

Of course, Heidi knew she would not carry out acts of vengeance, so her resentment manifested in other ways. She belittled Bob in her thoughts, heart, and conversations with friends and family. She spent hours mentally having long conversations with Bob and saying things she didn't have the courage to say aloud.

In time Heidi and her husband graduated from college and got great jobs. They moved far away from Bob and started a family of their own. However, Heidi still felt the far-reaching effects of Bob's cruel manner, and her resentment continued to be fueled by thoughts of him.

Toward the end of Bob's life, Heidi and her husband moved back in with his parents. At the same time, Bob was diagnosed with dementia, a condition that unfortunately intensified his ugly traits. He became completely uninhibited in his cruel taunts. Dina became more a slave to him than ever.

This time, sharing a home with Bob fueled a new flush of hatred in Heidi. She was convinced that there was no escape from his tyranny or the trap of her resentment.

One Sunday, Heidi reluctantly went with her husband to church. She was in no mood to be around people who, she felt, would never understand her hostility toward her father-in-law.

When the service was over, Heidi tried to make a quick escape, but she heard a woman calling after her. Only ten feet from the exit doors Heidi paused. *Ugh! Leave me alone!* she thought. The voice caught up with her. It was a friend. Immediately seeing Heidi's expression the woman asked, "How are you?"

Perhaps it was the gentle, concerned way the friend asked, but something in Heidi released and she started to unload about her anger. The two women sat down together, and Heidi spilled out the sordid details of what life with Bob had been like for the last eighteen years. Heidi ended by expressing how she wished that Bob would slip into a coma or die so the family could have some release.

The friend gasped, "But if he dies in a coma, how will he ever come to know Jesus?" Her words came straight from the throne room of God. They pierced Heidi's heart like a sword.

Though Heidi wasn't quite ready to forgive Bob, the conviction of God touched her soul. She looked at her friend and asked for prayer.

As they prayed, Heidi felt an immediate release of the hatred and vengeful thoughts she had harbored for years. The lump in her throat and the heaviness in her heart were gone.

Right then, Heidi's husband was walking up the church aisle toward her. She looked at him and said, "It's gone."

"What's gone?" he asked, totally unaware of the prayer that had taken place.

"I don't hate your dad anymore! It's weird but I feel like I'm not encumbered by this weight I've been carrying. I don't have to drag this thing around anymore. Let's hurry home to see if this is real. I want to check out how I react when I see him."

When Heidi arrived home, her father-in-law was already asleep.

Heidi had to wait until the next day to test her own reactions. Bob, true to form, barked a request for help from his chair. Normally, Heidi would have told him to get whatever he needed himself; instead, she walked toward him. She was sure that when she got close to him, she would revert to her old feelings and slap the demented man across the face. But she didn't. The nearer she came to Bob, the more peace she felt. The man who had terrorized and tormented her for 18 years became one of God's creations in her eyes.

Heidi asked him what he needed. He needed water. With pleasure, Heidi filled a cup with water and served it to her father-in-law. Heidi knew then that she was not just living a miracle—she was the miracle!

From that moment forward Heidi was able to serve her father-in-law without any residual feelings of hostility, anger, or vengeance. Heidi saw him in a whole new way. He was simply someone who desperately needed to be touched by God. Her heart became filled with compassion and grace for the man who was his own worst enemy.

Toward the end of his life, it was Heidi who became Bob's caretaker. Heidi would bathe him, change his diapers, and attend to his every whim. Often Bob would look up and ask her, "Why are you being so nice to me?" and Heidi would answer, "Because Jesus told me to. He loves you."

Heidi does not know if Bob ever gave his life to Jesus. She hopes that he surrendered to the love of Jesus. What Heidi is sure of is that she herself surrendered to the love of Jesus, and in so doing, gladly manifested Jesus's love and forgiveness to a very difficult and hardened man.

For so many years, Heidi thought that her freedom would be found in her father-in-law's punishment or death. However, she came to realize that her freedom came in releasing her vengeful thoughts and unforgiveness in prayer to God.

Jealousy

It is quite common for jealousy to turn into unforgiveness. Jealousy is defined as resentment against a rival or against another person's success or advantage. Like many women, I have struggled with this powerful emotion.

Did you catch the common denominator that runs through every seedling of unforgiveness? It is resentment. In this case the resentment stems from someone else's advantage, whether it be education, personality, position, possessions, good looks, or prosperity. The question arises in the heart: "Why should they have that advantage when I don't?"

The Bible says, "Wrath is cruel and anger is a torrent, but who is able to stand before jealousy?" (Proverbs 27:4).

It began very subtly for Jenna. When she was first introduced to Lynnette she was hopeful they would be good friends. Jenna had been urged by a mutual friend, a handsome young man from church, to befriend Lynnette, who was a new believer. Their first meeting was disastrous. When Lynnette was introduced to Jenna, she gave Jenna that up and down look that says, "You've been weighed in the balances and found wanting." Jenna was somewhat put off but ready to continue to try to win Lynnette over.

Lynnette was beautiful. Soon every young man that Jenna knew from church was talking about Lynnette. She began to confide in the man that Jenna was dating. Suddenly Jenna felt threatened. She began to watch Lynnette like a hawk.

She noticed things about Lynnette she had missed before. Lynnette was a flirt! Lynnette demanded all the male attention in the room. She was condescending to women. Slowly the case against Lynnette took shape in Jenna's mind.

Jenna tried to present her case to her boyfriend, Rick. He smiled, "Jenna, are you jealous of Lynnette?" Rick was trying to be cute but it only strengthened Jenna's resentment against Lynnette.

Jenna tried to ignore Lynnette but found her heart catching at the mention of her name. She wanted people to know Lynnette's true nature. Jealous? Not in Jenna's mind. Jenna considered herself discerning.

The problem was…Lynnette began to change. She was a new believer when Jenna first met her and still clung to some of the baggage of her old life. However, Lynnette was shedding the old baggage and growing in Jesus by leaps and bounds. If possible, Lynnette was becoming even more beautiful.

Jenna had been a spiritual leader in her church before and had the respect of the young women around her. Now Lynnette was gaining on her. Jenna was losing ground.

Eating dinner with her father one evening, something rude popped out of Jenna's mouth about Lynnette. Jenna's father looked crestfallen. "What is it?" Jenna asked noting her father's expression.

"I've just never heard you say anything so distasteful about anyone before. I hate to hear you talk like that. It just isn't like you."

"You don't know her, Dad. She's…not nice…she's a flirt…and…" Jenna stumbled over her words. Her dad looked both sympathetic and sad. Jenna began to cry. "What's wrong with me?"

"Jenna, do you need to forgive Lynnette?"

Jenna thought long and hard. It was true. She was holding resentment toward Lynnette. Perhaps Lynnette had rebuffed Jenna's first attempts at friendship, but she had reached out to Jenna many times since then.

Jenna went to her room and in the quiet solitude with God alone, she got to the root of the unforgiveness in her heart and the jealousy she felt toward Lynnette. Jenna forgave Lynnette before God, and soon they became dear and close friends.

Heart Injuries and Old Wounds

Without a doubt, unforgiveness can be triggered by injury and hurt. However, injury and hurt don't always turn into unforgiveness. There are some people who are experts at delivering the pain immediately to God and refusing to dwell on it. Then there are others who feed the injury and hurt so that it not only takes root, but it overtakes their entire heart.

Talia sat in church but though she was quiet, she wasn't listening to the sermon. Her mind was preoccupied with the latest conversation she'd had with her mom. In her mind she was tallying up all the rude things her mother ever had said or done to her. Talia could reach back to her childhood to begin numbering the offenses committed against her. Her mother had never hugged her. Her mother, steeped in her own self-image, had always treated Talia like more of an embarrassment than a daughter. The tallies increased.

She moved on to grade school. Her mother never attended an open house. Talia had moved from being an embarrassment to an inconvenience. More tallies. By the time the service was almost over, Talia hadn't heard a word that pastor had preached. She had spent the whole service feeding the appetite of her unforgiveness.

She had thought of new angles from which to see some of the events of her childhood. She was ready to share them with her husband over lunch. He would understand why she harbored anger toward her mother.

Suddenly the final words of the pastor's sermon passed through her ears and into her consciousness. "Pursue peace with all people, and holiness, without which no one will see the Lord: looking carefully lest anyone fall short of the grace of God; lest any root of bitterness springing up cause trouble, and by this many become defiled" (Hebrews 12:14-15). The pastor addressed the congregation, "Is there any morsel that you are holding onto that is jeopardizing your birthright? Are you holding bitterness against anyone? Is that bitterness worth jeopardizing your relationship with God?"

Did the pastor know the thoughts that had been forming in and poisoning Talia's mind? It seemed like he was speaking right to her. She suddenly realized that she had been feeding her resentment toward her mother one morsel after another. What would happen if she stopped feeding it? Talia decided to try. She prayed and asked God to help her remove the resentful thoughts toward her mother so she could stop dwelling on them.

When Talia stopped feeding those thoughts, she found that they dissipated. She still struggled with her mother at times, but she came to see that her mother deeply loved Talia in ways that she had never noticed. Though Talia's mother continued, at times, to hurt her feelings, Talia chose to treat them as isolated incidents and not feed them to the beast of unforgiveness. In time, the relationship mended. Today Talia and her mother are very close.

Proverbs 17:14 says, "The beginning of strife is like releasing water; therefore stop contention before a quarrel starts." If we can begin to recognize the seedlings of unforgiveness when they first enter our minds, it will be much easier to forgive. However, if we ignore these dangerous seedlings and give them fertile soil, water, and nutrients, they will grow into a tremendous plant that can only be uprooted with conscious effort and force. It is better to catch it at the beginning before, as the Proverb warns, it becomes "like releasing water."

Questions for Study and Personal Reflection

1. How would you define unforgiveness?

2. How would you define forgiveness?

3. What seedlings of unforgiveness have you experienced? How did you deal with them?

4. Which seedling do you consider the most dangerous?

5. Read Hebrews 12:14-15. Why do you think it is important to "diligently" check for "any root of bitterness"?

6. Provide an example of a time when resentment was fostered in your heart.

Prayer

Dear Lord,

Sometimes my desire for justice can turn into a thirst for vengeance. Help me trust You with every part of my life, including the wounds and the conflicts. I look to You, my Father of Mercies, to release me from trying to be judge and jury for those who have hurt me or those I love. You see the big picture. You know the hearts and needs of those involved... mine included.

Today, I release to You my anger and resentment so I may rest in Your peace and Your will. Show me how to live as a woman who seeks Your best in every circumstance. Each day, may I ask You to rule my heart and show me how to walk in Your wisdom. In Jesus's name, amen.

Chapter 4

The Consequences of Unforgiveness

It's always been hard for me to resist an invitation from my dad. This one was no exception! Picking up the phone, I heard his cheerful voice. "Hello, Angel!" It was his usual greeting. "There's a guy in the church who has a carpet store up in Fullerton. He has some great deals right now. I thought we could go up there together and look for some carpet for your house." Dad had become an active participant in fixing up the house we had just purchased. He knew Brian and I were shopping around for new carpet to go with the refurbishments we were making.

"Dick Lane is in the hospital up there, and I want to stop by and visit him. We could kill two birds with one stone."

Dick Lane? My mind reeled. Dick had been a close and trusted friend of my dad. He betrayed that trust when he cheated my father on a business investment. Dick chose to leave the church rather than apologize to my dad and pay back the money he had stolen.

"What happened to Dick?" I asked.

"He had a stroke and he's not doing so well."

"Does he know you're coming?" I asked.

"No, but I talked to his wife and she was really blessed that I wanted to see him."

Dad picked me up and we drove to Fullerton. Before we looked at carpet samples, we stopped at the hospital where Dick was recovering.

We made our way down long, sterile corridors to Dick's room. The door was open and Dick was sitting up in bed. I stood behind my dad as he gently knocked on the door to get Dick's attention. Dick looked up and began to cry.

Before we could enter the room Dick began to pour out his heart. "Oh, Chuck, I'm sorry. I'm so sorry for everything I did. You were the best friend I ever had. I wanted to come back to church. I wanted to make it right...I just never could do it."

Dad pulled a chair next to Dick's bed and sat down. He grasped Dick's hand in a manly way and said, "Ah, Dick, I forgave you a long time ago. The door has always been open."

The men then began to chat like old friends. They talked about their kids, their wives, and Dick's health. I was amazed. Dad's words and demeanor spoke volumes to me. I had a lot of closed doors in my past. There were people I had shut out of my heart and life. Here was Dad leaving the door open.

In the car on the way to the carpet store, I told my dad how proud I was. "Well, Cheryl," he said, "Jesus has never closed the door on us. He doesn't want us closing the door He's opened to others."

Dad had made the right choice by leaving the door open for reconciliation. When the time came, he found an opportunity for restoration and healing.

I know another man, about my dad's age, whose life is comprised of closed doors. He has shut one person after another out of his heart. Though the man grew up in a Christian home and sought a vocation in the ministry, he has wasted all his energies hunting down the "bad guys," trying to expulse them from his life. No matter what the offense, either real or imagined, he holds on to it tightly and never forgets. His family is estranged from him. He has very few friends. He blames his failed investments on those who gave him bad advice. When he was young, he made the fateful choice not to forgive. It became a forceful pattern in his life. Tragically, today he prides himself on his lack of forgiveness. He may have lost everything of value in his life, but he still treasures that list of offenses representing everyone who has done him wrong.

There are so many people who, like this man, set negative patterns in their lives. They become chained to those patterns of bitter attitudes, unforgiveness, and resentment and are often unwilling to make a change toward forgiveness. What follows in this chapter are the stories of the tragic consequences of those bad choices.

One Bad Choice After Another

For Anne, the choice began when she was still a girl. Unwittingly, she chose to ingest the unforgiveness she was fed by her mother. When Anne was only eight years old, her father abandoned her family. Anne's mother resented having to go back to work and provide for her daughter. She refused to nurture her daughter and instead fed her a steady diet of insecurity, fear of abandonment, and jealousy. Every day Anne heard the admonition, "Never trust a man. He will leave you for another woman."

Anne grew to resent everything in her life. She resented her first husband, who got her pregnant at 19. She resented the little girl she gave birth to and said even years later that she "was tricked into having her." Anne resented raising her daughter and the subsequent daughter who came along.

Anne chose to feed her daughters the same emotional diet she received as a child. She screamed, yelled, and intimidated her daughters, all the while remaining as detached as possible from them. She terrified the girls by telling them that when their father returned home from work, he was going to deal violently with them. No recriminations from their father ever occurred. It was just their mother's way of putting a wedge in their father's relationship with them.

When Marsha, Anne's oldest daughter, was 12, her father left. This confirmed Anne's own mother's mantra that "You cannot trust a man. They will leave you for another woman."

Marsha and her sister longed for a relationship with their estranged father. Their father went to court to ensure he had visiting rights and partial custody of the daughters he loved. The ordeal was extremely arduous for the girls. They had to explain to the court why they wanted a relationship with their father, and about their mother's verbal abuse. After Marsha testified, her mother had to be physically restrained. She screamed at Marsha in the hallway, "I hope you remember this day when you are in childbirth!"

It was impossible for Anne to sustain a healthy relationship with a man. She drifted in and out of one liaison after another. She became pregnant a third time by a man she was not married to. She gave the child up for adoption.

Anne savored each morsel of resentment in her heart. She drove everyone who tried to help her away—including two more husbands.

After Marsha became a Christian, she wanted to help her mother. Marsha chose to forgive Anne and reached out to her again and again. On one occasion Marsha took her mother to church. The woman sitting next to Anne, seeing the pain etched on her face, took her hand and whispered, "I love you." Big tears rolled down Anne's cheeks. Marsha realized that her mother was starved for love. Anne had never felt loved by anyone. She was abandoned emotionally by her mother and physically by three husbands, and even her two daughters were pulling away from her. It was impossible for Anne to love because she had never been loved. Marsha prayed for God to give her His divine love for her mother.

For over forty years Marsha tried to minister to Anne. Whenever she visited her bitter mother, Anne was angry and demanding. Marsha learned to be guarded in order to preserve her own spiritual and emotional welfare. Marsha did everything she could to help her mother. She asked forgiveness for any injury she may have caused. But Anne would redirect the conversation. Marsha tried probing her mom in order to understand the pain that caused such hostility to rage in Anne. Marsha came to dread their times together.

Marsha read in her Bible that Jesus was kind to the unthankful and evil (Luke 6:35). So with renewed vigor she tried to show her mother the transforming love of God. Marsha knew she couldn't change her mother, but she could do kind things for her and bless her.

Marsha and her husband went through a trying season of hardship. During that time, Marsha had to suspend her visitations to her mom until things could be worked out. Once the issue was alleviated, Marsha resumed her visits. Anne was angrier than ever. She acted out her bitterness and anger in visible and cruel ways. Then Anne spit out, "I hope something bad happens to all of you!"

Marsha tried to pity her mother. In a voice meant to be soothing, Marsha asked, "Is that the love of a mother?"

To this bit of correction, Anne responded, "You are not my daughter!"

"If you really feel that way," Marsha offered, "then don't call me again."

In that moment, Marsha heard the Lord's voice comfort her. "You're done, Marsha. You've done everything I asked you to do. I will take it from here."

Though Marsha knew that the anger and resentment Anne showed was a culmination of the hatred, bitterness, and hostility she held toward everyone that hurt her, it was still too much for Marsha to bear. Anne had added an unhealthy element to her marriage and family.

Anne is alone. She lives a very bitter life. She has no friends. Her own family waits for her to initiate reconciliation. Anne is resolute. She does not want to change. A series of bitter choices has left her a bitter old woman living a bitter life.

Marsha, on the other hand, has learned a valuable lesson from her mother. She has learned to keep short accounts and take every opportunity to choose to forgive.

Left to Herself

Penny was excited about her new house. It suited her needs and the needs of her husband and sons perfectly. It was great to move into a new neighborhood where all the houses were recently built, and everyone was meeting each other for the first time and building relationships.

Before Penny could begin to make friends with her neighbor, however, the woman came screaming out her front door at Penny's sons. Penny tried to find out what the boys had done, but the woman, Helen, was too upset to state any reasonable case.

A few days later the police arrived at Penny's front door. A complaint had been filed against Penny and her sons. One of the boys had tried to run the neighbor over in his car. Penny told the officer it wasn't true.

Another complaint came the next day. This time Penny and her family were accused of disturbing the peace. The officer came to check on the complaint. One complaint followed another. The police officers became a common sight at Penny's front door. She found herself opening the door with the words, "What have we done now?"

It wasn't just the complaints that came in rapid succession. So did the screaming fits and expletive language that would fly from her neighbor's house. Penny's dream house was turning into a nightmare.

Penny prayed and asked God for help. It hadn't been easy for Penny to turn each of her neighbor's tirades and complaints over to the Lord. But ones that had to do with her neighbor's attacks against her sons were the hardest to forgive. Penny kept making the conscious decision to forgive; however, something had to be done. An idea came to her mind. Her neighbor was English. Penny would prepare an English tea on a beautiful tray and take it next door.

Penny baked scones, made sandwiches, and boiled water for tea. She picked out a big tray and arranged everything in beautiful order. She covered it with a decorative tea towel and set out for her neighbor's house. She prayed as she walked and as she knocked on Helen's door.

When Helen answered the door, she was clearly shocked to see Penny standing there with the tray in hand. "What do you want?" she demanded.

"I want to have tea with you," Penny said gently.

The neighbor opened the door and gestured for Penny to enter. She pointed to a coffee table in the living room and Penny set the tray down. She pulled the tea towel away to reveal the beautiful ensemble that she had prepared. The neighbor visibly softened.

For the next hour the two women chatted like old friends. Before Penny collected the dirty dishes she asked her neighbor, "Can I come over again?"

"Please do," the neighbor responded.

It became a regular ritual between the two women on Wednesday afternoons. In time Penny learned that Helen was estranged from her children and husband. They continued to live in England, while Helen had moved to the States. Helen harbored resentment against each of her family members. While still living with her family, they had confronted her about her alcoholism. They had forced Helen to choose between a relationship with them and her alcohol. Helen denied that she had an issue with alcohol and refused to seek help. Her son, daughters, and husband, after years of begging, left Helen to the consequences of her actions.

Helen relished the self-pity she drowned herself in. She couldn't see her culpability in the circumstances that estranged her family. Penny realized that Helen was usually drunk when they shared tea.

Financial hardship hit Penny's family. She had to go to work. The weekly tea parties had to be postponed. At first they continued on a sporadic basis. But Penny, tired from work, soon stopped putting forth the effort.

Not long after, the police began to reappear at Penny's door. Helen again started screaming expletives at Penny's sons. "What happened?" Penny asked herself. She thought she and Helen were friends.

Penny marched over to Helen's house and knocked on the door. "Helen, what is going on?" she asked.

Helen stiffened. "You are just like everyone else. You left me. You just pretended to be my friend so I wouldn't press charges. Well, it's over! I'll see you in court!" Helen slammed the door in Penny's face.

Penny tried to reengage Helen. She left her sweet notes in her mailbox. She made another tray full of goodies, but Helen just screamed at her from behind the shut door. In the end, Penny just had to leave her neighbor alone. Eventually, she and her family moved away. There never was another point of connection or friendship with Helen.

There are too many stories like Anne and Helen's. I know men who hold their grudges more tightly than their wallets. They continue to inflict pain on themselves because of their refusal to forgive, but they view that pain as righteous indignation.

I have heard of a pastor who preached a sermon on "Why Forgiveness Is Not Necessary." Besides being an unbiblical and un-Christlike proposition, it is unhealthy theology. It is a misapplication of Luke 17:3-4: "Take heed to yourselves. If your brother sins against you, rebuke him; and if he repents, forgive him. And if he sins against you seven times in a day, and seven times in a day returns to you, saying, 'I repent,' you shall forgive him." The pastor asserted that forgiveness is only necessary if the person repents.

Jesus didn't predicate forgiveness on repentance. He forgave us while we were yet sinners (Romans 5:8). Jesus cried from the cross,

"Father, forgive them, for they do not know what they do" (Luke 23:34). Jesus forgave us before we even repented. Our repentance is our acceptance of what He has offered us. When we repent, we accept the forgiveness He has given us and subsequently we are freed from the heavy consequences of our sin.

In the same manner, we are to offer forgiveness to all who offend us. Our forgiveness cannot be predicated on their repentance. If we wait for offenders to repent, we will be left holding the bitter bag of unforgiveness in our heart.

The second problem with this bad theology is that God is the one who sets the standard for repentance. When my kids were little, after one of them would apologize to the other, I would often hear these words: "Sorry is not enough."

There are some people who will not accept any overtures of repentance. They will always demand more so that they can hold unforgiveness over another. While they wait for their requirements to be met, they will only find an increase in hostility, resentment, and anger. Chances are if the requirements are made, there will be a whole new list of unrealistic requirements waiting.

If you are waiting for someone to repent before you choose to forgive them, be careful that you don't begin to establish a pattern of holding grudges while you wait.

A pattern of unforgiveness is a dangerous thing. There are those who find themselves so hardened in the routines they have established that it is almost impossible to break free. It is better to stop the pattern while you still have the strength and resolve to do so.

Before we can conclude this chapter, I feel it imperative to give one last warning to anyone reading these pages who feels justified in retaining any hostility, animosity, grudges, and unforgiveness. Holding on to unforgiveness is a very costly choice.

When Being Right Gets Unhealthy

There are many people walking around in the graveyards of

unforgiveness who began their quest with a righteous cause. When their request for justice was not met immediately, they began to harbor resentment. The resentment soured in their system and released the deadly poison of bitterness throughout their body.

The story of a just cause turning to sinful rebellion and bitterness is found in the life of King David's son, Absalom. His tragic story is found in 2 Samuel chapters 13–18.

It was said of Absalom that of all David's sons he was the most handsome and admired. He had an engaging personality and was popular with the people of Israel. He had a strong moral sense and would often deliberate over the legal matters in Israel. He also was a caring big brother to his beautiful sister, Tamar. As one of the eldest sons of David, and the grandson of the king of Geshur, Absalom had a strong claim to the throne of Israel.

Absalom began his quest with a righteous cause. He was justly angry with his brother, Amnon. Amnon raped Absalom's sister Tamar. Absalom expected his father David to act righteously and punish Amnon for his heinous crime. However, David was delinquent in his responsibilities and though the matter visibly upset him, he pushed it aside and did nothing.

After two years of waiting for his father to take action, Absalom took judgment into his own hands. He held a party at his house and requested that all his brothers attend. At the party, Amnon was ambushed and killed by Absalom's servants. Absalom then fled to the kingdom of Geshur and lived there until he was summoned back to Israel at the request of his father, David.

Absalom returned to Israel and waited for his father to embrace him. After one brief meeting, David virtually ignored his son and treated him with indifference. It was not right.

During the next four years, a slow, burning rage festered in Absalom. He gathered an army together—an impressive array of men—and went to Hebron, where his father had first been made king. There, surrounded by two hundred men from Jerusalem and David's lead counselor, Ahithophel, Absalom was proclaimed king.

Absalom's anger was not subdued with the open rebellion against his father. He took his vengeance even further. He marched into Jerusalem, forcing David to abandon the palace and the city. Absalom then disgraced his father publicly before planning an assault against him.

The kingdom of Israel was divided between the men who were loyal to David and those who were loyal to Prince Absalom. The nation entered a grueling civil war in which the casualties numbered 20,000. Absalom was caught and murdered. His body was thrown into a large pit in the woods and covered over with a heap of rocks.

I have to admit that in the beginning of Absalom's story my sympathies are with the young, moral, and handsome prince of Israel. But somehow in the ensuing years, Absalom's unforgiveness toward his brother Amnon was so intense that it could not be pacified even by Amnon's death. The burning rage in Absalom became a self-destructive force with devastating consequences for the nation of Israel. Absalom began in the right, but because he allowed anger, bitterness, and unforgiveness to fester in his heart, his life ended in ignominy.

Absalom's tragic end serves as a warning to anyone who holds onto unforgiveness. The toll of holding onto unforgiveness is costly. It produces more than emotional turmoil. It has an adverse effect on one's mental, physical, and spiritual health. It truly hurts the one who holds it and nurses it more than the one to whom it is directed.

Holding anger, resentment, and an unforgiving attitude is simply not worth the toll it takes on you. For the sake of your well-being and health it is time to consider the path of forgiveness.

What Are Your Patterns?

Do you remember when you were a child and made an ugly face? Usually someone would warn, "Better watch out. If the wind blows while you are making that face, you will look like that forever!" That warning was enough to make me change my grimace into a smile. I did not want to spend the rest of my life with a frowning, ugly face.

Though we all know that the wind cannot freeze the expression on our faces into a look we will be cursed with throughout life, it is true that if we continually choose to be ugly and not forgive, we can settle into a bitter, lasting pattern. That undesirable pattern will be with us all our lives and leave us bereft, lonely, and desperately unhappy.

I meet people who begin their complaint about another person with the words, "I really love that person but…" I am always a little wary of this beginning. Usually what follows is long list of offenses the "loved" person has committed. I think it would be much more honest to say, "I really struggle with loving this person because of what they have done." An honest disclosure of our true feelings is the best base to work from. When we are honest with ourselves before God, He can work more effectively in us by helping us to move from recognition to choice.

In 1 Corinthians 13:4-8, Paul outlines the characteristics of love. These characteristics make a good litmus test for our claim about loving those we think we have forgiven. For the sake of an accurate prognosis, I have phrased the attributes of love as questions to ask ourselves.

1. Am I enduring this person's offenses with kindness?

2. Am I envious of that person's prosperity?

3. Do I feel compelled to showcase my own achievements in comparison to their successes?

4. Do I feel superior to the person I am offended by?

5. Have I behaved rudely toward them?

6. Do I keep a record of all the wrongs others have done to me?

7. Am I more concerned about my own welfare than I am about theirs?

8. Am I easily provoked by their behavior?

9. Do I wish them harm?

10. Am I glad when they fail or when others see them fail?

11. Am I happy to hear about their spiritual progress?

12. Am I loyal to them, even when they offend me?

13. Do I hope and want the best for them?

If you answer these questions honestly, you will realize that you need to love more and in various ways. The good news is that you are not alone. We all have to keep recognizing our insufficiencies and struggles. It is the recognition of our deficiencies that helps us to choose to forgive and seek God's help and power to do so.

The only way to fail the 1 Corinthians 13 test is to be dishonest in your answers and remain in denial about the true weaknesses of your heart. The love defined in this portion of Scripture is a love that is divine. Humanly speaking, it is beyond our grasp. This love requires an honest confession of the failure of the present feelings we possess and a reaching out in prayer for the divine love God wants to work in and through us.

We can set a good pattern of true love and forgiveness if we are willing to recognize when we lack this type of emotional connection with another person and ask God for His divine love to overtake us. When we get into the pattern of admitting our insufficiency and asking God for help, He strengthens us to love with His love.

Questions for Study and Personal Reflection

1. What adverse effects have you personally experienced from holding unforgiveness toward someone else emotionally, mentally, physically, and spiritually?

2. What warning do you derive from Absalom's story?

3. For what reasons would you encourage someone to forgive another person?

4. Read 2 Corinthians 2:10-11. How does the devil take advantage of unforgiveness?

5. Why is bitterness dangerous?

6. List the areas of love where you find yourself insufficient. Now give these same areas to God.

Prayer

Dear Lord,

I know there are patterns I have developed in my life to protect my heart and even to protect others that I care about. I see now that those are my way to stay in control and to build barriers between myself and the act of forgiveness. I don't want to hold grudges, become bitter, or distance myself from others or from You.

Soften my heart and my mind when I am reluctant to forgive someone in my life. Your gentle encouragement calls me to find freedom in this brave and important step. You are here for me, even in the midst of pain caused by another. When I forgive, I am resting in Your strength and not in my own. It feels so good to know that I am not alone and that Your grace is sufficient for me and for all Your children. In Jesus's name, amen.

Chapter 5

Why You're Ready to Forgive

Since you are holding this book in your hand, chances are that you are longing to find a way to believe you are forgiven or to find a way to do some healthy forgiving of others in your past or present. Maybe you are ready for both to happen and you are tired of feeling the weight of unforgiveness pressing you into unhappiness, shame, regret, and all those other emotional and spiritual pits we so easily can live in for years.

You have taken some important steps already, so take a moment to be glad for that and to rejoice in making progress. We are on our way to experiencing the benefits of living in grace and accepting God's great offer.

Forgiving someone is good for you. Holding on to unforgiveness extracts a heavy toll on your emotions, mental state, physical well-being, and spiritual life; however, forgiveness infuses those areas with light and life and hope.

This doesn't mean that the path and the personal work it takes to forgive is easy. The whole process can be quite arduous for people. But maybe it is a bit easier to begin the journey when we realize the dividends are worthwhile, healing, and eternal. Forgiveness is one of the best things you can do for yourself.

Let's take time to look at these areas of health and healing and to look forward to the benefits we'll experience along our path of learning to forgive and receive forgiveness.

Emotional Benefits

Forgiveness strengthens emotional bonds when it is extended in an ongoing relationship that you want to nurture. Think about a connection you have with a friend or your husband or a family member that involves forgiveness from and by both parties. It has likely been strengthened by the act of forgiveness. Trust can more readily form between people who bestow grace on each other.

Individuals who choose to forgive are better at resolving conflict, sustaining long-term relationships, and having overall better quality relationships than those who refuse to forgive. The following story about Barry is an illustration of how God can transform the hardest of hearts.

Barry grew up with a stepfather who was verbally and physically abusive. He felt he lived his life walking on eggshells around the abusive man. He never knew what would or wouldn't send his stepdad into one of his violent tirades.

While in high school and then well into his twenties, Barry's rage was evident every day. After he'd brush his teeth in the morning, he'd grip the sides of the sink with all his might and stare in the mirror. And every day, he would look himself in the eyes and vow that one day he would murder his stepfather.

Outwardly Barry looked like a calm guy, and very few of Barry's friends knew about the seething emotions inside. He used his inner rage as fuel for working out and soon became a star athlete at his school. He was handsome, well liked, and personable. He had many friends but he didn't feel a close affinity with any of them. At the end of the day, it was just Barry and his vow.

After Barry graduated from high school, he worked various jobs. He dated, but he never allowed a woman to get to know him very well. In the times of loneliness, he was frustrated by his inability to feel close to anyone; however, he accepted that he was not the type to settle down. Then one night, everything changed. It was the night Barry gave his life to Jesus.

Someone shared with him how he could have a relationship with God. The idea of being loved and known by God gave Barry a spark of hope. He jumped at the chance to find out how to develop this relationship and eagerly prayed to welcome Jesus into his heart and life.

He didn't feel an immediate difference after he prayed. However, the next day he could sense a real change in his attitude toward people. He felt a deep concern for his friends that he had never felt before. When Barry's curiosity about God became a thirst to know God, he developed a deep concern for the eternal welfare of others. He shared Jesus with his friends, and a great many of them became saved. They began to meet together regularly for prayer and Bible studies.

One day, Barry called his mom's house. His stepdad answered. It was the first time Barry had talked to him since he had become a Christian. Barry was shocked at the tone of his own voice. It was friendly and upbeat. It was then that he realized it had been months since he had repeated his vow into the bathroom mirror. Barry no longer hated his stepfather. The enmity was gone.

Barry began to notice that the detachment that once characterized his life was missing. In time he met a Christian girl and married. As I spoke with Barry, he expressed the joy of being very emotionally attached to his wife and kids.

Before Barry forgave his stepfather, it was impossible for him to form healthy relationships with others. His hatred for his stepfather sabotaged every relationship he had. Once he forgave his stepfather and received Jesus into his heart he discovered a new love and empathy for people. God gave him the freedom and gift of building deep, meaningful relationships.

Mental Benefits

Proverbs 23:7 reads, "For as he [a man] thinks in his heart, so is he." In other words, you are (or you become) what you think. When your thoughts are constantly negative, you become a negative person. In Matthew 12:34, Jesus said, "Out of the abundance of the heart the mouth speaks."

Have you ever had your mouth betray the feelings that were going on in your heart? I have! I was upset at a certain woman in the church for talking against me. (You will soon see the irony in this story.) I hadn't told anyone my feelings. Outwardly, I was treating her with deference and kindness.

However, one night when my kids were sick I had to stay home from church. After church, our friend Lizzy dropped in. This young girl who lived down the street often stopped by and was especially dear to both Brian and myself.

She was complimenting Brian on the service when something was mentioned about the woman that had upset me. From the couch I said some disparaging thing about her. It just popped out of my mouth.

Brian and the young girl looked shocked. "The main point of the message tonight was about why it is important to speak kindly about one another."

I was so ashamed. I was on the verge of tears. I realized that I had a heart problem. I confessed it to both of them because it was useless to cover it up. I prayed and God took care of it. Ouch!

That was one of the days that my mouth betrayed the true feelings of my heart. Here I was angry with this woman for talking about me, and what did I turn around and do? The very thing she had done to me. I said something distasteful about her.

The mental benefits to forgiving are numerous. First, when we get rid of those negative thoughts that are plaguing us, we are free to think good thoughts. Philippians 4:8 mentions the type of thoughts that are to occupy our minds. "Finally, brethren, whatever things are true, whatever things are noble, whatever things are just, whatever things are pure, whatever things are lovely, whatever things are of good report, if there is any virtue and if there is anything praiseworthy—meditate on these things."

There is no place for the thoughts that unforgiveness creates in this divine checklist. Unforgiving thoughts are not always true. They are definitely not noble. They are rarely just. They are not pure, lovely, or of good report. They are not virtuous or praiseworthy. Unforgiveness makes us think about the worst attributes in people, whereas forgiveness frees us to pray for God's greatest work and blessing to be manifested to people.

Unforgiveness is often accompanied by anger, bitterness, and resentment. So is it any wonder that there is a great reduction of these emotions in those who choose to forgive?

Gina found herself obsessed with Dory. It was hard to sleep at night. She kept thinking of the things Dory had said. Dory slighted Gina again and again. Dory made Gina feel so low. Gina tried to express those feelings to Dory in a friendly manner, but Dory turned the whole thing around and made herself the victim of Gina.

To make matters worse Dory began to write about Gina on Facebook. She never mentioned Gina by name, but everyone who had known them as friends knew exactly whom Dory was talking about. The portrayal of Gina was inaccurate and unflattering.

Gina would lie wide awake at night, exchanging sleep for imaginary conversations with Dory. She would toss and turn all night thinking of the things she wished she had said.

It became too much for Gina. She decided just to forgive Dory. She wrote her a note simply saying, "I forgive you." Then she laid it to rest. This infuriated Dory. But for Gina it was over. She had resolved to forgive Dory. She wouldn't read anymore of Dory's inflammatory posts. When Dory came to mind she would choose to forgive her.

It worked. Gina was able to sleep. Her mind was no longer

clogged with *she said this* or *she said that*. Instead she concentrated on the things that were true, noble, just, pure, lovely, and of good report.

Physical Benefits

For years Diane suffered with debilitating neck pain. The pain would become so excruciating that she would have to go to bed. When she first started having neck pain she thought it was a pulled muscle. However, after a time, the frequency of the recurring pain concerned her. Her doctor couldn't find anything wrong other than tightness in her muscles. Diane's pain continued to increase. She found it difficult to take care of her children and manage the house. She was constantly taking medication to help with the pain.

Then one day as she was lying in bed because of yet another episode with her neck, she prayed, "Lord, please heal my neck."

The name of a person arose in Diane's mind. She immediately felt her body tense. Then she felt the Lord whisper to her, "Forgive him." Diane chose to forgive. She felt her body relax. Then another person came to mind. Again Diane felt the tension in her body. Again she heard the Lord whisper, "Forgive." It continued all throughout the afternoon. One person after another came to Diane's mind. Each time she made the choice to forgive, she felt a physical release in her neck. Finally, the pain abated.

While I cannot guarantee that forgiving is a cure-all for your physical pains, I can tell you that many people I've spoken to will testify to a noticeable improvement in their health including:

- Lower blood pressure
- Lower levels of stress hormones
- Stronger immune system
- Decrease in stomach problems and digestive issues
- Healthier heart rates

- Fewer headaches

Now when my friend Diane experiences occasional tension in her neck, she does a quick heart check. If she finds any adverse feelings there, she surrenders it to God. According to Diane, she doesn't want to let anyone become "a pain in the neck" again!

The next time you sense your immunities down or your heart rate up, take a moment to do your own heart checkup with God.

Spiritual Benefits

When Peter asked Jesus, "Lord, how often shall my brother sin against me, and I forgive him? Up to seven times?" he probably thought he was being incredibly generous in his estimate.

Imagine his shock when Jesus answered, "I do not say to you, up to seven times, but up to seventy times seven" (Matthew 18:21-22).

Jesus wants us to forgive. He set the example for us when He freely chose to forgive us all our sins. Now He wants us to extend that same forgiveness to others.

I would like to suggest seven ways that forgiveness is beneficial to our spiritual lives.

One: Forgiveness is a great witness for Jesus.

When we forgive others, we are mirroring the actions of our Savior. Jesus forgave those who arrested Him, bound Him, abandoned Him, denied Him, ridiculed Him, beat Him, condemned Him, scourged Him, humiliated Him, paraded Him through the streets of Jerusalem, and crucified Him. Someone once suggested, "If Jesus had not cried from the cross, 'Father, forgive them, for they do not know what they do' we would never have been forgiven."

Some people struggle with sharing the gospel with others. They get tongue-tied when they try to witness. However, not all witnessing is done by word. Much of our witness is by our lives. When we choose to forgive we are providing a visible demonstration of the love and forgiveness that Jesus has manifested to us. You'd be surprised to find out how many people are watching your life. Forgiving others gives you the opportunity to showcase the grace of Jesus Christ in your life to others.

Two: Forgiveness prevents anything coming between Jesus and me.

Unforgiveness interferes with my relationship with Jesus. When I hold anything against someone else, I put that person between the Lord and myself.

There is a story about the English preacher C.H. Spurgeon that has been told and retold. A man standing on the street corner saw the preacher crossing a busy London road. Suddenly in the middle of the road, amidst carriages and horses traveling this way and that, Spurgeon stopped and put his head down. He stayed that way for a while. Then, lifting his head, he hastened his gait and crossed to the other side of the street. The man who was watching was curious about what he saw. He approached Spurgeon and said, "I noticed that as you crossed the street, you paused perilously in the middle of the road. Why did you do such a dangerous thing?"

With a smile on his face Spurgeon answered, "I felt a cloud pass between my Lord and me, and I couldn't go another step until the cloud had been dealt with."

Do you want a cloud between you and the Lord? Unforgiveness creates a dense cloud that can block our perspective of God. Forgiveness removes the cloud and allows us to have a clear picture of God and His grace.

Three: Forgiveness improves the quality of my prayers.

Jesus said, "And whenever you stand praying, if you have anything against anyone, forgive him, that your Father in heaven may also forgive you your trespasses" (Mark 11:25). The admonition from Jesus to forgive directly correlates with prayer. Forgiveness is to be a part of our prayer life. Unforgiveness left unattended will hinder and block our prayers.

Forgiveness allows us to pray unfettered by bitterness, anger, or prejudice. Forgiveness allows us to get to the pressing issues at hand without any preoccupation with the past or the person who has injured us. When we forgive we can press on to the greater depths of prayer.

Four: Forgiveness frees God to forgive me.

In Mark 11:26, Jesus cautioned, "If you do not forgive, neither will your Father in heaven forgive your trespasses."

God does not make us atone for our sins against Him. He provided atonement for our sins through Jesus. We cannot expect others to make atonement for their sins to us. When we have those expectations for atonement we are stepping into a position that belongs to God alone.

I freely admit that during my lifetime I have said and done a lot of stupid things. I am so thankful that God gave me gracious children and a gracious husband who have shown me forgiveness again and again. I certainly don't want to ever be in a place where I have to try to make restitution for every stupid thing that I have ever done. I am so blessed to know that the blood of Jesus Christ covers them.

I never want to jeopardize the status of having my sins covered by holding unforgiveness in my heart toward someone else. I want to forgive so that I can continue to be forgiven by God.

Five: Forgiveness keeps our faith unhindered.

In Mark 11 Jesus taught His disciples about the power of faith. He said to them, "Have faith in God. For assuredly, I say to you, whoever says to this mountain, 'Be removed and be cast into the sea,' and does not doubt in his heart, but believes that those things he says will be done, he will have whatever he says. Therefore I say to you, whatever things you ask when you pray, believe that you receive them, and you will have them" (Mark 11:22-24).

Right after this exciting proposition and promise, Jesus directs His disciples to forgive. The lesson is clear. Unforgiveness can diminish our faith.

When we refuse to forgive we are saying, "God, this one is too big for You. I will take care of it and hold on to it for You." Faith calls us to trust God and entrust to God. When we forgive we are entrusting every situation and person into God's hand. Faith is the power that God has given to us to see His will accomplished and the assurance that, "All things work together for good to those who love God, to those who are the called according to His purpose" (Romans 8:28).

Unforgiveness diminishes our capacity for faith. Not only does it crowd out the work of God in our heart, but it is also a constant attestation of doubt. It is the doubt that God can work even in this.

We want to see God work. The world needs to see God work. We don't want God's work diminished by unforgiveness.

Six: Forgiveness keeps us humble.

There is nothing more humbling than realizing that you need to forgive. The very act of forgiveness makes you feel vulnerable. But it is that vulnerability that keeps us humble.

Unforgiveness breeds pride and arrogance. The person who refuses to forgive feels superior to the offender. Isn't it true that you feel like you are a better person than the person who hurt you? The more a person refuses to forgive others, the more superior he feels to those that he refuses to forgive.

The whole notion that "I would never do to others what they did to me" is faulty. More often than not we find ourselves acting in the exact same manner as the person we refuse to forgive.

When we admit our mistakes and choose to forgive, we are in a better position for God to bless us. The Bible promises a blessing for the humble person. James 4:6 states, "God resists the proud, but gives grace to the humble." I don't know about you, but I don't want God to ever resist me. I want to be irresistible to God. I want His grace to pour out on me constantly. I think you want the same, right?

Seven: Forgiveness keeps us out of the debtor's prison.

Let's return for a moment to the parable in Matthew 18. Take a close look again at verse 34. The man who refused to forgive was "delivered…to the torturers until he should pay all that was due."

Certainly unforgiveness puts you in the prison of torture. In that prison you are tortured by emotional upheaval, constantly reminded of offenses against you. Ugh! What a prison.

It is this prison that Jesus wants to set you free from. He knows that the key out of this dungeon is to forgive others.

Jesus is not asking you to forgive others because they deserve it or have earned it. No. He is asking you to forgive because He has forgiven you and because He knows that forgiving others is in your best interest.

Forgiveness is good for you emotionally, mentally, physically, and spiritually. If you have struggled with the whole notion of forgiveness, I want you to consider the benefits you will derive from being willing to forgive.

Questions for Study and Personal Reflection

1. What benefit of forgiveness motivates you to want to forgive?

2. How do you see forgiveness as being beneficial to you?

3. Read Mark 11:22-26. What relationship do you see between faith and forgiveness? How do these verses minister to you?

4. What negative effects on your spiritual life have you experienced from refusing to forgive?

5. Write down a situation or person that you want to forgive.

Prayer

Dear Lord,

I look at my whole life and realize there are places of pain and conflict. Some wounds or negative attitudes have been with me for years. It gives me great hope to think of Your love and grace flowing through me and clearing away these places of pain, suffering, anger, and heartache. I want to experience wholeness and healing emotionally, mentally, physically, and spiritually.

Today I give to You all of my past grievances against others. They serve no purpose but to burden me and to litter my heart with debris. Cleanse me and create in me a pure heart, mind, and spirit so that I can become a new being in Christ. Let my life be about sharing freedom with others through forgiveness and through the sharing of Your Word and love. In Jesus's name, amen.

Chapter 6

How Do We Begin?

I remember cringing when a pastor said to me, "I find when I pray for my enemies, they become my friends." If only forgiveness was that easy! If only one prayer could change the direction of a relationship or the inclination of my own heart. Perhaps you've gotten some of the same advice! Perhaps, like me, you prayed and prayed for a particular person or to be free of unforgiveness only to sense that old feeling cropping up in your heart the moment their name is mentioned. For you, platitudes just don't work!

Often the situation is further complicated by the fact that the person you are praying for doesn't change, doesn't want to change, and in some instances is purposely trying to cause you injury. In those cases, expecting a friendship to develop from prayer alone can be lethal to any attempt to forgive. So what are we to do? Give up? No way!

Forgiveness is a process, and prayer is part of that process. There are, however, a few more steps to be taken. Just like climbing stairs leads you to a higher place, so taking the upward steps toward forgiveness will lead you to the higher place of freedom. Steps do not require a momentous leap. They are incremental. As you take one small step after another you find yourself at the top.

The same thing will happen as you begin the process of forgiving. It starts with just one small step—acknowledging the desire to forgive. I think you are reading this book because you already took that first step. There are only a few more left and you can do it. I can't help thinking of the blind man in Mark 8. When Jesus laid His hands on the man, he received only partial sight. "I see men like trees, walking." It took another touch by Jesus before the man could see all things clearly. The same could be said of all of us. We felt the touch of Jesus on us urging us to forgive. Now we just need that second touch, some very easy steps, so that we also can see all things clearly.

Forgiveness in Action

As Margaret drove her mother to the doctor one morning, she contemplated all the hardships of the recent months. Her father had recently died, relations with her sister had become hostile, and her mother was rapidly succumbing to Alzheimer's.

Margaret felt resentment build in her as she thought about how her sister offered no assistance but did offer a lot of criticism about the way their mother, Lillian, was cared for.

Lillian said very little. She had withdrawn further inside herself. She seemed to have trouble tracking conversations and was impatient with explanations. She preferred quiet to dialogue. Lillian had been a godly mother. For years she had been Margaret's counselor, confidante, and spiritual mentor.

Margaret recalled how Lillian had prayed her through every difficulty in her life. So now, as she was hurting deeply and in need of help, she felt alone and abandoned. There was no one for her to confide in. No one could possibly understand the depth of the emotional turmoil that brewed in her heart. Margaret could feel tears well up in her eyes as she tried to pay attention to the road ahead.

Suddenly from the passenger's seat of the car, Lillian spoke. "Why does your sister hate you so much?"

Margaret was astounded. She had no idea that her mother had any awareness of the situation between her daughters. She tried to console her mother by answering blithely, "I don't know."

Lillian was not through. "I know why. She hates you because she is jealous of you. She resents your happiness and contentment. She is so unhappy that she cannot be happy for anyone else."

"Yes. I suppose so," Margaret responded, aware that something amazing was taking place in the car.

Lillian continued. "Margaret, I have a favor to ask of you. Will you forgive your sister? Will you love her? Don't hold these things against her. Don't keep these things in your heart. Let them all go. Please? For me?"

Margaret stole a glance at her mother, who was now looking right at her. Her eyes seemed bright and alert.

"Yes. I promise. I will forgive and love her." Margaret nodded with conviction.

Suddenly the clouded look returned to Lillian's face. "Your sister hates you, Margaret. Did you know that? Why does she hate you?"

Margaret knew the familiar repetition of her mother's conversations, so she answered in kind. "I think she is very unhappy."

"No. That's not it. I don't know why she hates you," Lillian said before returning to her silent demeanor. The godly woman had returned for a moment to speak into Margaret's heart. God had met Margaret and had given her a message: Forgive.

Having made a vow to her mother, Margaret resolved to forgive her sister. She prayed and asked God to help her to let go of all the wrongs done to her. Unwittingly, Margaret had taken the very steps that led her into the freedom of forgiveness.

After praying, Margaret took the next step to erase the slate of offenses she held against her sister. She sat at the computer and deleted all the offensive, critical emails her sister had sent her. From there, Margaret sought to be vigilant about not letting unforgiveness gain a new foothold in her heart. Every morning she asked God to grant her the grace to keep forgiving old offenses and any new ones. Margaret continued to walk in the path of forgiveness, refusing to hold on to the past hurts.

Though Margaret's sister became more belligerent and greedy as life unfolded, Margaret remains free and happy. God's grace even enabled Margaret to shower her sister with empathy and love at Lillian's funeral—an amazing gift Margaret knew only happened because she recognized the need to forgive her sister and took the steps, with God's help, to do so.

Perhaps the thought of forgiving the offender in your life seems overwhelming. Maybe you have tried and failed. That's all right. Today is a new day and God's mercies are new every morning. Let the gift of grace and the treasures of forgiveness take root and grow in your life.

As we walk through each of the steps to forgiveness, may you be encouraged by stories of others who made this journey and leaned into God's strength for their every need.

Step 1: Recognize the need to give and receive forgiveness.

There are many people who are fostering unforgiveness in their hearts but are in denial of the bitterness they foster. The funny thing about bitterness in that the one who holds on to it is also often blind to it.

Bitterness is like bad breath. Everyone around you smells it, is repulsed by it, and knows you have it. Only the one with the bad breath doesn't know he or she has it.

That's how it was for a woman I know named Carrie. Carrie had problems with her brother. In fact, she had a whole list of issues with her brother dating back to when they both lived at home with their parents. There was the time that he got the neighborhood boys to throw dirt clods at Carrie when she was all dressed up to go to a party. There was the time he lied about her and got her in trouble with the neighbors. There were numerous times that he had trashed her room, taken her belongings, and lied about it. There were other things too...too personal and painful to publicly acknowledge, but that filled the deep recesses of her heart with anger and bitterness. She would not forget. Ever.

Growing up, Carrie made sure to maintain a certain distance in her relationship with her brother. Whenever she was forced to see him at a family gathering, he was sure to do or say something that would only add to the list of offenses already stored in Carrie's heart.

Carrie hoped never to have to be in the same proximity as her only brother ever again. But that was not to be. Carrie's mother's health began to fail and she had to move back to the town where her brother lived to help take care of her.

A close family friend named Barbara came to visit Carrie's mother. Afterward, this godly woman took Carrie aside and said, "Carrie, your mother is failing fast. You and your brother need to decide on what type of health care plan you will implement."

Carrie unintentionally grimaced at the mention of her brother. The woman noticed and asked if something was wrong.

"No. Well, yes. I can't work with my brother. I will have to do this myself."

The woman looked at Carrie with understanding eyes. "You will have to work with your brother for your mother's sake."

Carrie's body language communicated her disgust at the idea. She stepped away from Barbara and shuddered.

"Oh Carrie," Barbara said in a soothing voice. "We need to pray. Carrie, you are bitter toward your brother."

Carrie denied the accusation emphatically. "Bitter, no. He is a terrible person and totally unscrupulous, but I am not bitter. I dealt with my feelings about him a long time ago. I rarely think about him. It's just that this whole thing with Mom is what I'm upset about. I really don't want my brother around my mother. I don't think he's safe."

Barbara looked sympathetic. "Carrie, would you be willing to pray with me?"

Carrie agreed to pray. She loved Barbara and she didn't want to appear uncooperative or unappreciative. The older woman took

Carrie's hand and began to pray against the bitterness lodged in Carrie's heart.

Carrie found herself resenting Barbara's prayer. It made her uncomfortable.

Then Barbara prodded Carrie to pray and confess her bitterness. Carrie was sure that her emotions were due to her knowledge about her brother's character and had nothing whatsoever to do with bitterness. She demurred.

Barbara pushed Carrie a little harder. "Carrie, you need to release the bitterness."

Now Carrie was getting annoyed. She wanted this ordeal to be over. She decided to confess to bitterness just to please Barbara. And that's when it happened. The moment Carrie asked the Lord to deliver her from bitterness, the floodgates opened and the sorrow and anger that had been pent up for years poured forth. She found herself sobbing. Barbara held her. "It's going to be all right now, Carrie. You'll see."

Carrie left the meeting, not quite sure of herself or what happened. She still wasn't ready to admit that the emotional ordeal had to do with her having bitterness. However, there was a change in Carrie that was undeniable. The mention of her brother's name no longer moved her. She was able to converse with him and make plans for her mother's welfare. No, he hadn't changed and Carrie had to be careful, but she didn't mind the precautions.

Are you bitter? Does the mere mention of someone's name upset you? You might want to ask an honest friend if they think you have a problem with another person. Here are a few questions to help you discern whether you are reluctant to forgive someone. This is the first step toward ridding your life of resentment. Are you ready for some heart-to-heart honesty? Okay. Here we go.

1. When the subject of forgiveness comes up, is there a person who immediately comes to mind?

2. Can you recall, at any given moment, more than three things that person has done to injure you or others?

3. Do you struggle with sleepless nights thinking about this person?

4. Do you want to stay informed about what that person is up to? Do you try to find out what they are doing and what they are saying?

5. Do you feel the need to set everyone straight about the *true* nature of that person?

6. What is your body language communicating when that person's name is mentioned? (Do you grimace, recoil, stiffen, or tense up?)

7. Do your friends think you have a problem?

8. Do you talk negatively about this person more than once a day?

9. Do you rehearse and rehash the events of previous days, weeks, months, years?

10. Do you feel the need to prove your innocence or victimization?

If you answered yes to even one of the questions, it's time to recognize your need to forgive so you can move forward in the journey toward release. If you are unsure of the condition of your heart, pray like Carrie did and allow the release of unforgiveness to take place. Carrie is glad she did. Today she readily admits that she was set free when she prayed with Barbara.

Step 2: Make the choice to forgive.

I have a friend who has struggled with forgiveness. During one of our conversations about life and faith, I asked her to share with me the story about how she forgave her mother.

She responded, "I don't think I've fully forgiven her yet."

"Okay, then what about the woman you used to work with?" I countered, offering another suggestion.

She shook her head. "I don't think I've completely worked through that one yet either. However, I did forgive my father-in-law. I can tell you that story."

"I thought he was dead."

"He is. I think that is why I am walking in victory."

We both laughed.

My friend did realize that she was still "in process" when it came to forgiving a few people. There are a lot of people on the road to forgiveness who don't realize how much progress they've already made or that they have a ways to go. Why? Because they consider forgiveness a one-time event and expect to be totally over the hurt, anger, and resentment they have carried in one fell swoop of the Spirit. Though that has been the experience of a few people I know, it is not the case for the vast majority of believers. Forgiveness, for most of us, is a process. Like peeling an onion layer by layer, forgiveness is often multilayered.

As a pastor's wife, I have talked with and prayed for many women who have felt the urgency to forgive someone, but also felt unable to do so. Doreen was one of those women. During a time of prayer at a women's retreat she approached me and said, "I know I need to forgive my husband, but I can't. I keep trying but the anger flares up again and again."

I had one simple question to ask her. "Do you want to forgive?"

She nodded her head, "Yes, I do. I desperately do."

The next thing I asked might seem strange to you, but I have found that it is a vital question to ask. "Why do you want to forgive him?"

Doreen looked a bit taken aback. She thought for a moment or two. "Because it is interfering with my relationship with God."

"Then you are not choosing to forgive him because he deserves it but because you don't want anything to interfere in your relationship with God?" I took Doreen's hand and, looking into her eyes, I said, "Let's give that man to God. But I want you to know, you have already begun the process of forgiveness. You are here by choice, asking for prayer, because the desire of your heart is to forgive. You have already chosen the right road and now you just have to continue down the path."

Many people I have talked and prayed with, like Doreen, have begun the forgiveness process without realizing it simply because they don't feel a complete release, or they still feel some sense of angst when the offense or their offender's name is mentioned.

I like to tell these individuals that they've made the first crucial step by choosing to forgive. Getting to the "why" of forgiveness is vital. Rarely does an individual need to forgive someone who is sweet, kind, and non-offensive. Usually the struggle to forgive revolves around someone who is insensitive, selfish, or unloving and has caused injury, pain, and suffering. So an obvious reason to forgive such a person won't likely be "because they are good and deserving."

We have already addressed how forgiveness is beneficial for our hearts, relationships, marriages, physical well-being, and mental health. However, the greatest reason for choosing to forgive is because Jesus told us to. Over ten times in the Gospels Jesus commands us to forgive.

When I was a child I found that if my dad said something once, he probably meant it. If he said it again, he definitely meant it. If he said it a third time, I needed to remember it. If he had to repeat it a fourth time, it was a lesson for life.

So we choose to forgive because this is the will of our Savior. We choose to forgive because Jesus has forgiven us.

One day when I was a little girl I was due for some hefty discipline. I don't remember the offense. I was only four at the time. My dad sat down with me and before proceeding he asked me, "Cheryl, do you know what the Bible says about this?" Dad fully expected me to quote Ephesians 6:1 ("Children, obey your parents") or some such passage.

Dad says he was totally taken aback when I looked up at him and with tear-filled eyes said, "Be kind to one another, tenderhearted, forgiving one another, even as God in Christ forgave you." Even at a young age, I knew quoting Ephesians 4:32 was the wise move.

And sure enough, Dad forgave me that day and I got off without any punishment. Why? Because God had forgiven him for Jesus's sake. In the same way, we forgive others because God has chosen to forgive us, not only because of what Jesus has paid, the penalty of our sins, but also because Jesus wants us forgiven. And Jesus wants us to choose to forgive.

Step 3: Pray and give it to God.

Alexander Pope certainly got it right when he wrote, "To err is human; to forgive, divine." Forgiveness requires the divine element of God's help and grace. Prayer is first the surrendering of my heart and will to God. In prayer I release the offender and the offenses to God. The liens I hold against someone become His liens. I cancel that person's debt against me by giving that debt over to God.

Second, prayer supplies me with God's divine power and grace to walk in the spirit of forgiveness.

Many women, after making the choice to forgive, feel that decision challenged. For example, during the prayer time at a women's retreat, some participants will confess and lay their unforgiveness or bitterness down. They receive the release that comes through prayer. However, when they go home, that decision is threatened by old thoughts and maybe even new offenses. Sometimes women discover another bit of damaging information about the offender. Or maybe they run into that person at the store or at church and the encounter doesn't go well.

When such causes for assessment arise, these women second-guess whether they really did lay their unforgiveness at the foot of the cross. Is the bitterness still there?

They chose to forgive, but now they need to call again on the divine power of God to continue to ratify that choice. Prayer invites God into our hearts and minds. Only God can purify our minds and fill them with the right thoughts and clear our hearts of blame and other emotional ties that don't allow us to forgive.

When we humbly go before God and seek and receive His forgiveness, we are reminded how powerful and transforming mercy is. We are reminded that we are blessed with the opportunity to bring to Jesus our transgressions as well as our need to forgive others and all that stands in the way of us doing so.

Step 4: Clean the slate.

Clearing the history of another person's transgressions against us is the step that follows prayer. If you have recognized the need to forgive, chosen to forgive, and prayed for God's strength, yet continue to recount all the wrongs committed against you by the other person, you still have steps to take.

I know people who hold on to old letters or emails in which some insult or derogatory thing was said. They think they need these as proof of the offenses made. More often than not, the insults are between the lines and are only apparent to the one who struggles to forgive. The problem is that holding on to letters or other records of another's failings only keeps us in bondage. We don't move forward, and we don't reap the rewards of a forgiving heart.

My friend Gloria was in an abusive marriage for years. Though Gloria's husband came to faith in Jesus later in life, he was still difficult to live with. Gloria made the choice early on to forgive him. Walking in that choice took a concentrated effort and lots of prayer on Gloria's part. She shared this wisdom with me. "In my experience with Carl, after I forgave, I had to choose not to 'dwell on the offense.' I sometimes needed to go back to God and say, 'Lord, I chose to forgive Carl. I choose to not think about that offense any more. It is covered by Your blood and I choose to forget.'"

Gloria found that allowing herself to "relive" or "revisit" the offenses only brought her more pain and thwarted her progress on the road to forgiveness. The devil would use her visitations with the old offenses to drag her back into bitterness, resentment, self-pity, and self-justification.

You must cancel the debt by erasing the debt. In New Testament times, debts were reckoned and recorded on wax boards. When the debt was paid the board was erased. Consider your offender's debt paid by Jesus.

Let's look at this through the lens of metaphor. Imagine someone crashes into your car intentionally. They aren't willing to pay for the damages done to your car. However, a wealthy man who witnesses the wreck offers to take your car to his mechanic and restore it to even better condition than it was prior to the incident. The wealthy man is true to his word. Your car is returned to you in perfect condition. There is no need to seek out the rude fellow who hit you. It is better to be done with him and simply enjoy your car. The damage is repaired and you are better off than you were before you were hit.

This is what it means to erase the slate. God has paid for their offenses. The offender owes us nothing. It is better to be done with him or her and enjoy the new life that God has given to us in Christ Jesus!

Step 5: Be vigilant to guard your heart from unforgiveness.

There will be roadblocks on your path to forgiveness. Prepare yourself for the obstacles ahead. It is important to realize that this is a spiritual journey toward victory. The devil doesn't want you to make it to the end.

Consider the damage he can do by keeping you from victory:

- He can render your Christian witness ineffective.

- He can continue to torment you with the injury that was done to you.

- He can upset you at any given moment by the mention of the offender's name.

- He can isolate you.

- He can make you despair of ever having victory.

We read in 1 Peter 5:8-9, "Be sober, be vigilant; because your adversary the devil walks about like a roaring lion, seeking whom he may devour. Resist him, steadfast in the faith."

You must remember that the devil is able to put thoughts into our minds. We are told in 1 Chronicles 21:1, "Now Satan stood up against Israel, and moved David to number Israel." And John 13:2 reveals that the devil already put it into the heart of Judas to betray Jesus.

Yes! You must be vigilant even against your own thoughts and your own heart. Not every thought and emotion you have is safe. Any thought that draws you back into remembering what was done against you is not safe. Any thought that suggests you dwell on and explore, delve into, or reanalyze the offender or the offense needs to be taken immediately to Jesus and wiped out. Any temptation to add new tallies to the offender's crimes or start a new list of offenses needs to be resisted.

In 2 Corinthians 10:4-5 we are warned, "For the weapons of our warfare are not carnal but mighty in God for pulling down strongholds, casting down arguments and every high thing that exalts itself against the knowledge of God, bringing every thought into captivity of the obedience of Christ."

Be on guard for any thoughts that suggest you take a step backward on your path to forgiveness or lure you to the dark corners of resentment. Present these to God in prayer and commit to being in God's Word daily so you are defending your heart against falsehoods and unforgiveness with the power of God's truth and clarity.

Step 6: Keep walking and living in grace.

Recently, I experienced a situation that upset me. I replayed the incident frequently in the days that followed and I dwelled on my personal injury and the injustice of the situation. As I started to consider it yet another time, I heard the Lord speak to my heart: "Put the thing down. Put your hands up in the air and back away!"

That was exactly what I had to do. I laid the issue down before the Lord. I put my hands up in the air and surrendered the situation and my thoughts to God. Then I backed away. After that, I refused to pick it up again as I went on a wonderful ministry adventure to Australia with my husband. During the trip, the only thought I had about the entire event was that I was so thankful I had given it to God. I didn't give the situation any more power or pull in my life. And because I had done that, I was able to minister and fellowship and also praise God without the burden of an unforgiving heart.

God has good things ahead for you. Keep walking on the path to victory. Take inventory of all that God has done for you. Don't let anything or anyone slow your pace as you march on toward triumph!

In the chapters ahead you will find the amazing stories of men and women just like you who struggled to forgive. They were set free and are well on their way to victory—and you can be too!

Questions for Study and Personal Reflection

1. What signs of unforgiveness do you recognize in your life?

2. What has previously held you back from making the choice to forgive?

3. Walk through the steps to forgiveness right now. Think of something specific you need to forgive and make this important journey now:

Step 1: Recognize the need to give and receive forgiveness.

Step 2: Make the choice to forgive.

Step 3: Pray and give it to God.

Step 4: Erase the slate.

Step 5: Be vigilant to guard your heart from unforgiveness.

Step 6: Keep walking and living in grace.

4. You might want to make copies of the simple declaration: "Lord, I choose to forgive _____ for _____. I choose to not think about that offense anymore. It is covered by Your blood and I choose to forget."

5. Make a list of all the good things God has done for you. See if you can add a new thing each day to this list.

Prayer

Fill in the blanks of this simple prayer. Pray it several times as you lift up different people and circumstances to God.

Dear Lord, help me to forgive_____. I surrender the whole situation to You. Now I ask for the grace to walk in the victory of forgiveness. In Jesus's name, amen.

Chapter 7

Forgiving Ourselves

The woman came up to the front of the church for prayer. Her head was bowed in shame and she refused to make eye contact. "I just can't forgive myself," she said, barely above a whisper.

"But Jesus has forgiven you everything! His blood is so powerful that there is no sin that can resist His cleansing strength!"

For the next twenty minutes or so, the woman confessed one sin after another. Each time she confessed, I would say, "Covered! Wiped out by the blood of Jesus. Next..."

There are many women who struggle to forgive themselves. They are the offender they battle to forgive. Their own offenses continually haunt their mind and condemn them.

Taking the Steps to Forgiving Yourself

The steps to forgiving yourself are the same as the steps toward forgiving another. However, the questions that lead you along the path are a little bit different. Here are some to consider:

1. Do you berate yourself constantly for things you have done or said?

2. Are you constantly apologizing to others?

3. When people share a story, do you process it personally,

assuming they're trying to convey a secret message to you?

4. Do you feel unworthy to have a certain position or blessing?

5. Do you have trouble receiving compliments?

6. Is there something in your past that you blame yourself for letting happen?

7. Are you afraid if others find out what you did, they will not forgive you?

If you answered yes to one or more of these questions, then it's time to recognize your need to forgive yourself. It doesn't matter if you are guilty or not guilty. God has forgiven you. You must apply the forgiving work of God to your own life.

Now you must make the choice to forgive yourself. That's right—forgive yourself! Now, repeat after me: "I forgive myself because Jesus has forgiven me. I accept that I am washed clean by His blood, not because I deserve it, but because He has so much love!"

We all stumble and make mistakes. We are all sinners by nature. In fact it is impossible to make it through life without injuring or hurting someone else. James 3:2 states, "We all stumble in many things. If anyone does not stumble in word, he is a perfect man, able also to bridle the whole body."

After you have chosen to forgive yourself, it is time to pray and ask God to ratify that choice. Ask God for the grace to forgive yourself. And just like the steps in forgiving others, you need to wipe the slate clean of the wrongs you have done. It does you no spiritual good to berate yourself over the past.

Years ago my husband and I were giving one of our famous lectures to our teenage daughter over something she had done. With haughty indifference she said to us, "That's in the past and we don't talk about the past."

At the time I had no idea how intently her five-year-old sister had been listening. Just a few days later, my youngest daughter was spending time with her grandparents and they were having a gentle argument. Kelsey suddenly spoke up and, incorporating the same haughty air of her older sister, stated, "Grandma, that is in the past and we don't talk about the past." My mom and dad burst into laughter.

My mom called me minutes after the incident to tell me. "But you know, honey," she said, "it really convicted me. She was right. I was bringing up something from the past that I needed to leave in the past." Out of the mouths of babes...

In Philippians 3:13-14, Paul had this crucial piece of advice: "Brethren, I do not count myself to have apprehended; but one thing I do, forgetting those things which are behind and reaching forward to those things which are ahead, I press toward the goal for the prize of the upward call of God in Christ Jesus."

Paul the apostle put the past behind him so that he could continue down the path of victory that God had for him. As believers, we must put the past in the past, forget those things that are behind, and make our way toward the upward call that God has for each of us.

The same vigilance needed to safeguard the resolve to forgive others must be incorporated in forgiving ourselves. Every condemning thought must be brought into the captivity of Jesus Christ.

This vigilance is a little more difficult because there is a fine line between knowing my undeserving estate and living in condemnation. It is important to remember that you are qualified by Christ, not by your own merit. Colossians 1:12 states, "the Father...has qualified us to be partakers of the inheritance of the saints in the light."

When thoughts of being unqualified for grace arise you must reckon yourself as qualified by God through Christ. People tend to think that being hard on ourselves is ultimately holy or pious. But true spiritual wholeness involves us seeing ourselves complete in Jesus because of what He has done on the cross for us. "You are complete in Him, who is the head of all principality and power" (Colossians 2:10).

Recognizing that you are complete in Christ and forgiven is not presumption; it is a declaration of praise for what God has done. From this point you need to walk in victory. God has wonderful plans for you. He has placed a call on your life.

Before we move on, consider for a moment the condemnation Paul could have wallowed in. Before he met Jesus on the road to Damascus, Paul had violently persecuted the church. He had dragged men and women out of their homes and thrown them in prison. He had consented to and enabled the stoning of the martyr, Stephen. Had Paul not reckoned his sins covered by the blood of Jesus and chosen to put the past behind him, he would never have been such an effective tool for the spreading of the gospel.

God used Paul in amazing ways. Paul not only took the gospel to Asia and Europe, but he also established several churches, strengthened the faith of believers, and wrote inspiring epistles that continue to minister to many generations of believers.

Keep walking on the road to victory, for God has great plans for you.

Laurie's Story

By the time I got to know Laurie, she was a brilliant Bible teacher and leader in the women's ministry. I had no idea that she had past shame or ever felt any condemnation for her mistakes.

One day over coffee, Laurie confided in me that she had sat at the back of the auditorium when she first started attending Bible study. She refused to join in a group. She was sure if her story was known she would be asked to leave.

Laurie has been unfaithful to her first husband. They were both believers and Laurie had even grown up in a Christian home. She never planned to be unfaithful. Craig was the dashing single man at their church. All the unattached women at the church were agog over him. He had a charismatic smile and a dynamic personality. He also could sing and play the guitar. Was it any wonder so many women were smitten?

Laurie thought Craig was good-looking but she was perfectly content in her marriage. Her husband was an ample provider. He was kind, and best of all, he adored Laurie.

Laurie never expected to be attracted to Craig. She certainly never thought she would ever have an affair with him, but that is what happened. It all started with a light flirtation over Bible translations, of all things. Craig had asked what Bible she used for her devotions. He said that he had overheard something she had said and liked the way she phrased it. Laurie handed Craig her Bible and in the process their hands touched. Laurie felt a tingle run up her spine. She looked at Craig and saw him blush. She knew he felt it too. She spent the rest of the evening stealing furtive glances at him. She thought he was staring at her.

Once home, she couldn't get Craig out of her mind. She looked him up on Facebook. She found an excuse to send him a message about her Bible. It grew from there. For quite a while, Laurie considered the flirtation harmless. She justified it in her mind. Yet she found herself becoming emotionally distanced from her husband. He appeared so boring and steady compared to the excitement she felt around Craig.

One day Laurie came home after a secret rendezvous with Craig and found her husband on the couch with his head in his hands. When Laurie approached him, she found he had been crying. He told her that someone at church had informed him of the affair. Laurie was shocked to hear the word "affair." She knew the relationship had gone way too far, but until this moment she had been so caught up in the thrill that she had failed to recognize it as sin.

Laurie found it difficult to end her relationship with Craig.

Though they called it off, the attraction between them continued. Finally, Laurie's husband had enough. He asked Laurie for a divorce. It wasn't until the divorce process started that the full brunt of what Laurie had done hit her. She longed to have her innocence back. She wanted desperately to erase all the damage and pain she had caused to her husband, the church, family, and God. It was too late.

After the divorce, Laurie and Craig officially ended their relationship. Resentment was the only feeling that remained with Laurie toward Craig.

Laurie was utterly alone. She felt she couldn't return to church after what she had done. She was afraid to pray and yet she desperately needed God to intervene in her life.

A few years later, Laurie met Mac. He wasn't a Christian but he was a great guy and he loved her. She fell in love with Mac. A few years after they married, Mac came home with some astonishing news: He had given his life to Jesus Christ. Mac was enthusiastic about his new commitment to Jesus. He wanted to start attending church as soon as possible. After only a few weeks at their new church, Mac got involved in serving. He was growing rapidly in the faith.

In the meantime, Laurie lingered behind. She was thrilled for Mac and she loved watching him mature in Jesus. Her own thirst for God was insatiable. She desperately wanted what Mac had but felt that she had blown it too badly. She had sinned against God in commiting adultery as a Christian. In her mind there was no going back. She felt like an outsider in church and desperately wanted in.

One Sunday morning, the woman sitting next to her pointed out the women's Bible study to her. "Oh no. I couldn't possibly go," Laurie said.

The woman wasn't finished. "Sure you can. I'll pick you up."

Under the pressure of the kindly woman, Laurie agreed to go to the Bible study. She loved it.

Laurie was an extremely gifted woman. She had wonderful

communication skills. She was a great administrator. She could see how her skills could really be an asset to the women's ministry but she held back. She figured that she had disqualified herself early on from ever being used by God.

So she quietly attended the Bible study lectures, did her homework, and went home. After a year, she was invited to join a discussion group. Again pressure was applied and Laurie succumbed. She loved dialoging with the other women about the wonders they discovered in God's Word through their weekly study. Laurie's insights were so profound and her spirit so lovely, she was recommended for leadership.

Laurie declined when she was asked to lead, and after pressure to reconsider was applied, Laurie felt she had to disclose her reason for refusing. She dredged up the sordid details of what had taken place fifteen years prior. She expected to be asked to leave. Instead Joanna, the women's ministry administrator, looked at her and asked, "Haven't you forgiven yourself yet? It's time to give yourself and all your gifts back to God for Him to use as He wants to. Remember, you've been bought with the price. You are not your own. Everything you have belongs to God."

Laurie asked for time to pray. When she went home that night, she realized that she hadn't forgiven herself for the damage she had done in her first marriage. Though she had asked God's forgiveness, she had never forgiven herself.

Laurie looked up 1 Corinthians 6:20, "For you were bought at a price; therefore glorify God in your body and in your spirit, which are God's." Laurie let the power and truth of this verse sink in. Laurie didn't belong to Laurie anymore. She belonged to Jesus. He had forgiven her and she owed Him everything. Now He wanted to use the gifts He had given her. Laurie surrendered it all to Jesus.

The next day Laurie called and accepted the position offered to her by the women's ministry leadership.

Sitting across from her I could barely believe the story that poured out. "Are you kidding me?" I exclaimed. I couldn't believe that this vibrant, beautiful, selfless woman had ever struggled with forgiving herself.

Today Laurie continues to be a blessing to the women's ministry.

Have you been holding back from serving at church because you feel disqualified by sin, weakness, failings, or past troubles? Have you been hiding your gifts and denying your calling because you feel unworthy? If so, take a long moment to remember that Jesus Christ purchased you. He paid for the forgiveness of your sins with His precious blood. Now all that you are and have belong to Him. You owe it to Jesus to use your gifts for His glory.

Katie's Story

The best way for you to know Katie's story is to let her tell you herself. I met Katie over ten years ago. I only knew her as a kind, diligent, and engaging employee at the church. However, over the years, I would hear tidbits here and there about her testimony.

Five years ago our church decided to do a huge renovation on the main sanctuary. It was long overdue. To facilitate services the church pitched a huge tent on the playing field on the front of the property. It was impossible to conduct the women's Bible study as usual, so we asked several women to share their testimonies on Friday morning. Katie was one of the women who shared. This is what she said:

"I wasn't born with the ability to forgive anyone. I had to be taught. In fact, I wasn't even aware that forgiveness meant life. For me the whole concept of forgiveness meant death.

"I had been married for eight wonderful years to my husband when I fell into the sin of adultery. We had three children at the time, ages five, three, and one. I thought I had pulled it off without anyone knowing. I pretended to be a faithful wife and cheerful mommy. However, within a month's time, my husband found out about the affair. He was so despondent that at work one day, he put a gun in his mouth and pulled the trigger. He left me a note informing me that he knew about my adultery. I was left as a disgraced widow with three small children to care for all by myself. I rightly blamed myself for all that happened.

"When you're responsible for someone else's death, the guilt is overwhelming and consuming. I tried to erase my guilt and shame with drugs and alcohol, but they barely numbed the pain. Every time I was sober the shame would come rushing in and overwhelm me all over again. So I ended up taking more drugs and drinking more alcohol. This led to an hourly addiction of smoking pot and meth and then pouring vodka into a Slurpee cup to disguise the problem from my kids. The addiction turned me into a mean and angry mother with a short fuse.

"Many times I wanted to take my own life. I didn't think I deserved to live. I made plans to sit in my car in our closed garage and turn on the engine. But before I turned the ignition key, I went inside the house to grab a marijuana cigarette, thinking if I got stoned it would ease the fifteen-minute wait until the intoxicating fumes suffocated me. But I never did turn the ignition on. When I went inside the house, someone knocked on my door.

"Then the day came when I was arrested for drug possession. I blamed God for everything. I blamed Him for my husband's death. I blamed Him for my addiction. I blamed Him for my incarceration. I blamed Him for having my kids taken away. And then I blamed Him for letting me live at all.

"Standing in the jail's shower I railed against God. Then, right in the middle of my tantrum, I ran out of things to blame God for and I started sobbing and crying in relentless fits of pain until I could cry no more. Within moments of this tirade, two words came forth:

"'I'm sorry.'

"Then it began to flow like a torrent from my lips, 'I'm sorry, God! I'm so sorry!' I had never thought of God before as anything but an impersonal moral authority. Surprisingly, though, the next words that I uttered were, 'Papa, help me. Papa, I'm sorry.' In my heart I knew I was to blame for everything that had happened.

"As I stood in the shower, water rushing down upon my head, I knew that in that moment God had forgiven me and I had accepted His forgiveness.

"Since that day, I've stumbled upon the true meaning of the word 'receive.' There is one synonym in particular that I really like. It is the word *welcome*. On the day I accepted God's forgiveness, I put a welcome mat in front of the door of my heart and I said to Jesus, 'Come on in.' From that day forward, I've never been the same.

"God's forgiveness led to a transformed and restored life! Because of God's grace and love for me, He took my sin of adultery and washed me clean. He altered the consequences of my sin and gave me beauty for ashes.

"Today I'm able to shout for joy because of the peace that God has given me since I welcomed His forgiveness. Miraculously, by God's grace, I'm remarried to a godly man who has adopted my three children as his own. I never expected God to be able to use me as He has. However, God has not only used my testimony to help others but as a family, with my husband and kids, we serve in the ministry together. My husband and I even serve in the drug and alcohol ministry to help others discover the forgiveness of God in their own lives—and to welcome it."

Before Katie received God's forgiveness she couldn't forgive herself. She never imagined that she would be doing anything productive for anyone else. The pain and injury she had caused others ate away at her. She was her own worst enemy.

Then one day, what began as a tirade against God ended up with Katie receiving God's forgiveness and then forgiving herself for all the damage she had done to others. God not only forgave her and restored her, He also put her into the ministry.

Like Paul the apostle, Katie can proclaim, "And I thank Christ Jesus our Lord who has enabled me, because He counted me faithful, putting me into the ministry, although I was formerly a blasphemer, a persecutor, and an insolent man; but I obtained mercy because I did it ignorantly in unbelief. And the grace of our Lord was exceeding abundant, with faith and love which are in Christ Jesus. This is a faithful saying and worthy of all acceptance, that Christ Jesus came into the world to save sinners, of whom I am chief" (1 Timothy 1:12-15).

Have you thought your life was beyond repair? Have you given up on yourself? God has not and will not ever give up on you. He wants you to receive His forgiveness. God wants you to forgive yourself and enter into the good things He has for you. It's time to get on the road to victory and use your God-given gifts to bless others on that same road!

Questions for Study and Personal Reflection

1. Have you ever felt disqualified from serving God because of sin?

2. What are some of the pestering thoughts that condemn you?

3. Make a list of all the things you feel disqualify you from being used by God. Then take a red pen and write "Paid in Full" over each item. Reckon each item as forgiven by the blood of Jesus Christ.

4. Take inventory of the gifts God has given you. What are some of the talents He has enabled you with?

5. Write a prayer committing yourself and each of those giftings to God for His use.

6. Write out 1 John 1:7-9. Circle every word that pertains to your forgiveness. How will you appropriate 1 John 1:7-9 into your life?

Prayer

Dear Lord,

I come to You today with a great need for Your love and grace. I am Your child and yet I put myself down, I force myself to recount my past sins again and again, and I don't extend grace to myself. I have become frugal with the love You shower upon me, Lord.

Give me a heart that is quick to gather the gifts and the joys that are a part of my life. Clear my mind of the long list of faults I carry around with me. I have made mistakes. I have sinned. And I have come to You with a heavy heart to ask for forgiveness. Now I am free. Totally free. May my attitude toward myself and others reflect this amazing truth. In Jesus's name, amen.

Chapter 8

Forgiving God

It seems almost blasphemous for someone to say that they need to forgive God. However, if we deny the reality that we hold Him ultimately responsible for all that goes on in our life, we will never know the true freedom of forgiveness.

Blaming God for the ills of life has been an inclination of man since the beginning. In the book of Job, we read that Satan's violent acts against Job's children were blamed on God. The reality was that Satan had asked to test Job's faith in God by destroying all he had (Job 1:6-15). When the news was given to Job concerning the loss of his sheep and servants, it was reported in this way: "The fire of God fell from heaven and burned up the sheep and the servants, and consumed them; and I alone have escaped to tell you" (Job 1:16).

When it comes to bad things happening in our lives, one of the first questions we ask is, "God, why did You allow it?" Many of us know the stories of God acting to save His people. In the Bible we read of God's divine intervention on behalf of His saints. God delivered the Israelites from Egypt. God saved David from the spear of King Saul. God rescued Daniel from the wrath of Nebuchadnezzar. God freed Peter from the prison...and the list goes on.

It makes sense that our minds go to, "Why not us?" But when we are stuck in that line of thinking, we aren't paying attention to how God moves in people's lives in many of the other stories—the stories of God not delivering His children "from" but "in" the circumstances.

Shadrach, Meshach, and Abednego were not spared from the fiery furnace of King Nebuchadnezzar! However, they were miraculously sustained in the fiery furnace. Daniel, the aging prophet of God, was not spared from the lion's den. However, he was divinely preserved in the den of lions. God does not always spare His precious children the ordeal of heartache, pain, and suffering. We will never understand the "why" this side of heaven. In our finite imagination, we simply cannot grasp the glory of heaven or what waits on the other side.

Paul suffered tremendously during his lifetime. As a minister of God, he was not spared from hardship, stripes, prison, whippings, beatings with rods, stoning, shipwreck, perils, betrayals, weariness, insomnia, hunger, thirst, cold, nakedness, or a chronic condition that weakened him. Yet Paul would declare, "For our light affliction, which is but for a moment, is working for us a far more exceeding and eternal weight of glory" (2 Corinthians 4:17).

Paul could not justify the suffering he experienced on earth, but he declared that heaven would more than make up for any suffering experienced on earth.

Don't Trade in the Truth

How do we view the times when believers doubt God? A commonly aired grumbling is, "If God is a God of love, why does He allow pain to exist?" There probably isn't a Christian on earth who hasn't once asked the same question about a tragedy, loss, or life upheaval: "Why, God, why?" If we dig a little deeper, this question can actually lead us to richer truths about God's nature.

My father is famous for saying, "Never give up what you know for what you don't know." There are a lot of things I can't understand. Though I know sin has corrupted the glory and beauty of God's original plan for earth and men, I still sometimes struggle to understand why God allows evil to harm His children. So I take time to pray, to be in God's Word, and to seek a greater understanding of my heavenly Father. When I cannot understand the *why*, I fall back on *what* I know about Him.

1. God is good (Psalm 119:68).

2. Heaven is real and will more than make up for the suffering on earth (Revelation 21:4).

3. God can use even this for my good and His glory (Romans 8:28).

4. God knows my pain and understands me (Hebrews 4:15).

I know these truths are absolute. The *whys* I cannot possibly understand without seeing the other side, which is heaven. Paul the apostle said, "For now we see in a mirror, dimly, but then face to face. Now I know in part, but then I shall know just as I also am known" (1 Corinthians 13:12).

If God didn't allow evil, He would not be just. Have you ever thought about it like that? God must allow us to live with the choices we make and the inevitable consequences that follow. Also, it is impossible for us not to be touched by the consequences of bad choices made by others. The price of living in a fallen world, in part, is being affected and injured by the rebellion of others. That rebellion has brought the consequence of sickness, disease, war, crime, violence, neglect, and a host of other harmful ills.

Secondly, God allows suffering because if it weren't for pain on earth, we would never long for heaven. God has something better in store for us. That is a truth and it is also an unknown, because we don't know what it will be like to be in God's presence for eternity. However, we do have faith in the One who is with us in the middle of hardship and who never abandons us, even when we express our doubts.

God Wants Our Honesty

It is no use trying to hold secret resentment toward God. He knows our every thought. He knows when we are harboring unforgiveness toward Him. He wants us to confess to Him all our doubts and accusations. He's got an answer, a comfort, and a release for each one. David exhorts us in Psalm 62:8 to pour out our hearts to God. When we pour out the entire contents of our hearts to God, sometimes unforgiveness against God, hidden in the crevices, pours out too.

Once we recognize and confess that we are holding resentment or anger toward God, He is able to do an amazing work in our hearts. The stories in this chapter have to do with women I know who admitted to God that they held Him accountable for the suffering in their lives. That blame kept them from fully trusting and surrendering their lives to Him. They could not progress on the road to victory until they recognized this truth, confessed to God, and prayed for the grace to forgive. When they did, something wonderful happened.

Lottie's story

As strange as it may seem, Lottie needed to forgive God for making her the way she was. Lottie is absolutely beautiful. Her smile brightens an entire room. Her sense of humor is engaging and quirky. However, for years, Lottie couldn't see any of the wonderful attributes God created in her. Lottie was only aware of her inadequacies and weaknesses.

Isn't that just like so many of us? We rarely notice our beautiful qualities that others are drawn to, but we are quickly able to identify our worst qualities.

At times Lottie would rail at God for her shyness, awkwardness, and her feelings of displacement. During her personal tirades, Lottie's heart would cry out, "Why did You make me the way I am? You did this to me!" After these episodes, Lottie would go on a binge, gorging herself with food. According to Lottie, it was the "nice girl" way to rebel.

One day it dawned on Lottie that she needed to forgive God for making her the way she was. Perhaps her perspective wasn't right, but we don't always approach God with the right perspective. So instead of shouting at God about her circumstances, she found herself saying, "God, I forgive You for making me the way I am. I don't belong to me. You created me for Your purposes. If You can use me for Your glory, here I am."

Guess what happened? God accepted Lottie's forgiveness. He took her up on her offer. God began to create in Lottie a new life of grace. God used Lottie's shyness, awkwardness, and feelings of displacement to help her to understand the feelings of other women just like her. As Lottie surrendered everything to God, she was healed of her eating disorder.

Lottie still struggles with occasional feelings of inadequacy. However, the episodes are fewer and farther between. When she feels one coming on, she confesses all her feelings to God and she dedicates even her weaknesses to Him. Today, believe it or not, Lottie leads the women's ministry at her church.

Are you blaming God for making you the way you are? Have you tried to hold Him responsible for your inadequacies and the things you hate about yourself? It's time to have a long conversation with God. Admit to your feelings and give Him absolutely every emotion in your heart. God will accept your forgiveness. In place of your inadequacies, He will give you His sufficiency. Then you will discover the grace that Lottie found and with Paul proclaim, "Therefore most gladly I will...boast in my infirmities, that the power of Christ may rest upon me" (2 Corinthians 12:9).

Addie's Story

Tears formed in Addie's eyes as we spoke. Ten years after losing her darling little Amanda, Addie's pain was still strong. "You have to connect the dots, though," she told me as she gave me permission to use her story. "No one will understand the decision James and I made unless they connect the dots."

Addie had been changing Amanda's diaper one morning when she felt a lump protruding from her tummy. Addie made an appointment with the doctor and took Amanda right in.

Tests were done and it was soon confirmed that Amanda had a cancerous tumor growing on her liver. For the next five months Amanda received chemotherapy. She endured every painful and uncomfortable procedure with grace and patience. She rarely cried. In her free moments, Amanda behaved and looked like any other healthy child. She ran, played, and teased her older sister.

The tumor shrunk to an operable size and Amanda was admitted into the hospital. Before the surgery, Addie and James committed their precious little girl to Jesus for His very best.

A few hours later they were informed that the surgery was successful. The tumor was removed. However, as Amanda was in recovery she developed an infection. She died as a result of the negligence of the nurse attending her.

In the midst of Addie and James's grief they applied to the state for an investigation into Amanda's post-operative care. Grief brings forth extreme emotions. Addie and James experienced deep sadness one moment and then anger and frustration in the next moment. As they poured out their sadness before God, they couldn't help but ask, "Why?"

In their time of anger they questioned the competency of the people who cared for Amanda. The nurse was found to have acted negligently and placed on discipline. He was not allowed to have children under his supervision.

Even after this chapter was closed, there was more anger and disappointment to deal with. Addie and James forgave the nurse for what had happened. However, Addie realized that in her heart she hadn't forgiven God for "dropping the ball" and not safeguarding her little girl. Growing in Addie's heart was a deep sense of distrust of God and strong suspicions about God's goodness.

The following year, a friend of Addie's had their first grandchild delivered by emergency C-section. The attending doctor had checked the baby's heart rate and made the call to deliver the baby right then! Everyone was relieved that the doctor had made such a wise call. Addie rejoiced with her friend, who had been so anxious about the safety of her grandchild. Addie thought about God's intervention, so obviously seen in the safe delivery of this little child. This begged Addie to ask the question, "But where were You, God, when I needed Your help?"

The words of Psalm 121:1-3 came to her mind, "I will lift up my eyes to the hills—from whence comes my help? My help comes from the Lord, who made the heaven and earth. He will not allow your foot to be moved; He who keeps you will not slumber." As Addie began to converse with God, she found herself accusing Him of not being there when she needed Him and not doing what she asked Him to do. She confessed that she was angry with Him for healing and saving others but letting little Amanda die.

As Addie poured out her heart to God she suddenly had a realization of who she was talking to. This was God, who created the heavens and the earth. This was God, who skillfully made the human body. This was God, who sustained all of creation. This was God, who had been faithful to protect, deliver, provide, and care for Addie all throughout her life. How could His loving care fail? Addie didn't fully understand, but she knew she had to make a decision. She would either have to forgive God and accept what He had done, or she would continue to grow bitter and angry and insist on her right to have life the way she thought it should be.

In that moment, Addie chose to surrender herself to her Father. Addie forgave God.

Addie was comforted to read, "He shall preserve your soul" (Psalm 121:7). She clung to that verse and its truth. She came to realize that each man, woman, and child is not just flesh and blood; they are eternal, spiritual beings. Amanda is in heaven. There she is happy, whole, and in the presence of Jesus.

Addie discovered that God is ultimately the determiner of the things that happen. Blaming God only kept her from receiving the divine comfort she so desperately needed. When Addie released her unforgiving heart to God, she was able to continue down the road to victory. It is a road which will ultimately lead Addie into the very presence of Jesus, where she will see her precious Amanda sitting at His feet.

Liz's Story

When Liz was ten years old, her father abandoned the family to marry another woman and raise her two sons. Liz's mother made a meager salary so there was little money for life's essentials. Their meals often consisted of meat patties and cottage cheese. While they struggled, Liz got word that her father and his new family ate lavish dinners at the finest restaurants. The situation was even more glaring at Christmas. Liz and her sister received two humble gifts while her stepbrothers opened heaps of expensive ones.

There was no money for school clothes. Often Liz would have nightmares of showing up to school with nothing on. Her father's abandonment and the poverty she was experiencing began to affect Liz's outlook on God. She believed in God and she loved Him. But she had a serious problem with God not providing better for her family. How could it be that she and her sister, who loved God, were barely surviving, while her ungodly dad, who did everything wrong, was living the high life?

Over and over Liz's dad would let her down. He made many empty promises that he had no intention of fulfilling. Like so many women, Liz came to equate her earthly father with her heavenly Father.

God was working in Liz's life during this time but she couldn't always see it. Liz's mom could sense her anxiety and began to pray in earnest. Over the course of her growing up years, God supplied Liz and her sister with many miraculous provisions. They received gifts, were awarded prize money, won games at birthday parties, were given beautiful clothes, and even collected the prizes for many contests they entered. People would anonymously send her family checks in the mail. God even miraculously provided the tuition so Liz and her sister could go to a Christian school.

Though they struggled merely to live a simple life, God was there taking care of their every need and safely guiding them through every crisis.

In the meantime, Liz's father continued to make more empty promises. Liz's excitement over receiving a car from her father turned to dismay when she stepped out of her house one morning to drive to school and found that her car was being repossessed.

It wasn't until late in high school that Liz began to make sense of it all. After a series of nightmares and fears overwhelmed her, Liz realized that she had been holding unforgiveness against God. She was angry with Him for letting her dad abandon her family, the lack of money, and all the hard times. In the midst of crying angry tears, Liz asked God to forgive her for holding a grudge against Him. God met the teenager in that moment and released her from all the pent-up tension and stress she had been holding. As she spent time with God, her eyes were open to see how much better off she was in the care of her heavenly Father than with her earthly one. She realized that through her circumstances and hardships, God had given her a heart of compassion for others that she wouldn't have had otherwise. Even when other people let her down, she knew that she could put all her trust in a loving heavenly Father.

The evening of her prayer, Liz was also able to forgive her father for his neglect and selfishness. This newfound attitude of forgiveness allowed Liz to love her father and see him through God's eyes. She was able to be with him when he died and assure him that he was forgiven for all the injury he had caused.

The lessons Liz learned the night she forgave God are still with her today and continue to minister to her when finances get tight and crisis hits. Liz knows that she has a heavenly Father who will miraculously provide for her and her family.

Ruth's Story

When Ruth was only seven years old she was sexually abused, raped, and used for child pornography. For years afterward it affected the way Ruth viewed herself and the way she viewed God.

Ruth could not come to terms with why God seemingly abandoned her during that time. She never shared this accusation with others. To anyone who knew about her past, Ruth would explain that God had been there with her, comforting and protecting her through the ordeal. But in her heart, she felt sick when imagining God in those rooms watching every awful, painful thing that happened to her and doing nothing to stop the abuse. At other times Ruth chose to believe that God was not present when she was abused. No scenario for what had happened to her when she was a little girl eased her pain. She was miserable. And though she tried to shut the trauma out of her daily thoughts and remove it from her memory, it affected her in every conceivable way—physically, mentally, emotionally, and especially spiritually.

Ruth became upset with God each time she read a story in the Bible that mentioned a woman being abused. She accused Him of hating women and allowing them to be victimized. In private she held on to this view of God and the deep anger that accompanied it. Then, at a retreat, Ruth was asked to pray for the women there. Ruth tried to listen to the women that streamed forward for prayer, but her own issues were gnawing at her. Ruth was unable to contain the emotions that were welling up inside. Suddenly she realized she was angry against God about every area of her life. It was not only the scope of the anger that amazed her; it was the strength of it.

An older woman approached Ruth right at that moment. "Are you all right?" she asked. Suddenly Ruth began to convulse with sobs until she was finally able to form words. Then the floodgates really opened up. All the pain, anger, and hostility Ruth had been holding came pouring out. The woman held her hand and listened until there were no more words left for Ruth to say. There was no condemnation. The woman prayed over Ruth.

The next morning Ruth sat in the back of the sanctuary. She wanted to be alone. The worship leader invited everyone to close their eyes. When Ruth closed her eyes a scene began to appear in her mind's eye. She saw herself flying through the sky with Jesus. He held her tightly. She looked down from the heights and saw the house that she was molested in. She looked back at Jesus. He was crying. They swooped down together onto the house and flew through the rooms. Ruth saw the whole scene playing out before her, but she was above it all, safe in the arms of Jesus. They grieved together over the loss of her innocence and she could feel her Savior's pain.

Next she saw a large book. Each page contained a story from her life played out in living color. Page after page turned before her and she remembered things that she had suppressed, forgotten, or hidden in the darkest recesses of her mind. In each page, God would write Himself into the story. Ruth was unsure where the chapters were leading, but she saw an epic novel being created. Suddenly she realized it was the story of her life. And as that story unfolded, Ruth found herself forgiving God for every wrong and evil thing that had ever touched her life. As she forgave Him, the story took on more colors and became a grand adventure. The vision seemed to go on for hours, when in reality it was only minutes.

Ruth knew that God had done something in her life in that moment. She waited in anticipation for the speaker to share. The topic the woman discussed was how God was writing the story of each woman's life. Ruth was astounded!

That weekend, Ruth forgave God.

Ruth left the retreat a changed woman. She now volunteers for and gets involved in the women's ministry. She has renewed transparency with her friends. And she has developed a deep sense of compassion for other people. Best of all, she has a peace about how God cared for her and will continue to care for her through all the pages of her story.

Refusing to Forgive God

Sadly, there are people who experience anger toward God but do not find their way toward peace and understanding as Ruth did. When anger continues, the unforgiveness will not only destroy the quality of one's life on earth, but it will jeopardize their eternal welfare. The price is just too steep.

Tim was angry with God. When I asked him why, he practically spit the answer out. He blamed everything that went wrong in his life on God. God withheld the girl he loved from marrying him. God crashed Tim's car when he was driving. God let Tim's parents get a divorce. There wasn't one bad thing in Tim's life that he didn't blame on God.

As his litany against God seemed to be nearing an end, I asked him, "So, do you believe in God?"

"Of course I do. Who else is ruining my life?" Tim was no atheist but he wasn't a believer either. Tim was mad at God. In his anger he took no responsibility for any of the problems in his life. According to Tim, he was a good guy being persecuted by God.

Tim had a distorted concept of God. He expected God to bless him constantly, whether or not Tim served or honored Him. Tim wanted God to give him all the best in life and never withhold anything from him.

Tim wanted to control God.

I tried to explain how a God that Tim could control and order around could be no God at all. "Do you really want the God who created and maintains the universe to condescend to your limited understanding? Do you want Him to base His decisions on your momentary whims and wishes rather than on the eternal welfare of all mankind?"

Tim looked a little sheepish. He didn't really want to consider what I was saying. He wanted someone other than himself to blame. God was an easy mark.

However, blaming God is simply not a wise move. Blame turns quickly into bitterness, and bitterness hardens the heart. A heart hardened against God is a heart that removes itself from all the comforts and promises of God. Does life seem bad now? If you turn away from God, it will get indescribably worse.

The time has come to trade what you don't understand about the sufferings of this life for what you do know about God. God is good. God has a great, benevolent plan that cannot be understood this side of heaven.

If you have held God accountable for the things that have gone wrong in your life, it is time to forgive God and start receiving His comfort and grace, allowing them to flow through your life again.

Questions for Study and Personal Reflection

1. Describe a time, if any, that you felt let down by God.

2. What issues in your life have you blamed God for?

3. Read 2 Corinthians 4:17-18. How might the glory of heaven make the sufferings on earth pale in comparison?

4. Why do you think it is a wise idea to forgive God?

5. Take a moment to pour out your heart before God. Tell Him all the things that have upset you, including the issues you don't understand. Don't forget to forgive God for the things you don't understand.

Prayer

Dear God,

I search my heart and I find residual anger at You for times when life was really hard. I give that anger to You and I seek Your forgiveness and healing. I know I have blamed You when the consequences of my own actions or the actions of people I love affect lives in negative ways. Instead, I should be running to Your shelter and sitting at Your feet to ask for guidance and hope.

Show me the way to live, Lord. Show me how to release any blame I hold against You now. I don't want anything to come between me and Your incredible healing love. I will rest in what I know about You. And I know You to be faithful, loving, forgiving, and overflowing with mercy. I love You, God. In Jesus's name, amen.

Chapter 9

Forgiving Others

The prayer the Lord Jesus taught His disciples to pray serves as an important model for every believer. Contained within the requests of this short prayer are the very essentials that should be resident in every prayer. It is a prayer that if prayed from the heart and with full understanding will put us in the spirit of forgiveness.

> Our Father in heaven,
> Hallowed be Your name.
> Your kingdom come.
> Your will be done
> On earth as it is in heaven.
> Give us this day our daily bread.
> And forgive us our debts,
> As we forgive our debtors.
> And do not lead us into temptation,
> But deliver us from the evil one.
> For Yours is the kingdom and the power
> and the glory forever. Amen.
> (Matthew 6:9-13)

First, there is the acknowledgment that God is "our Father." We share the same Father. Unforgiveness is always isolating. It makes us want to pray "my Father" and exclude anyone else from the benefits of God's fatherly love. When we acknowledge that we share the same benevolent father, we understand that He wants all of His children to behave, be blessed, and be of one heart toward Him.

The second acknowledgment in this prayer is the acknowledgment of the power of God's name. Within the name of God—I AM WHO I AM—is contained all the resources that we need for life and godliness. God's name is the declaration of His benevolent character and attributes, His willingness and desire to share those gifts with us, and also the great wealth of His resources.

The first request is for the kingdom of God to come. The full implications of this request will not be realized until Jesus returns to rule and reign on the earth. When that happens, every wrong will be made right. However, there is a secondary application for our lives today. God wants to set up His kingdom in our hearts. He wants to be Lord and ruler of our hearts. When we pray for God's kingdom to come, we are asking God to reign in our hearts. God desires to reign in our hearts before He reigns in this world.

The second request in this prayer is for the will of God to be accomplished. God's will is not only good; it is of the highest good. This means that the things God allows, whether we understand their good purpose or not, have a higher order, divine purpose, and an eternal reward. This understanding and request helps us to relinquish the bad things that happen to us to God's capable hands. God's will is always done in heaven, and heaven has no sorrow, pain, or injury of any kind. In heaven there is healing and comfort, glory and perfect understanding, joy and love. This is the expectation of God's will. So when God's will is brought to bear upon our earthly circumstances we can expect healing and comfort, glory and understanding, joy and love.

The next request is practical. God understands our physical needs. He knows that we need to eat, drink, rest, be clothed, and have all the other necessities of life. God created us, and as our Creator, He knows exactly what we need. Jesus said, "Your heavenly Father knows that you need all these things" (Matthew 6:32). Jesus instructs us to pray for our *daily* bread. God wants us to depend on Him and come to Him in prayer every single day for all of our needs.

Notice the request that follows our necessary bread: "Forgive us our debts." Every day we are to acknowledge that we need the continual forgiveness of God. Every day we are to recognize that we are debtors to God because He has forgiven us through the death and sacrifice of His dear Son. This understanding and appeal keeps us humble before God. It reminds us that we are debtors to God's grace and goodness.

What follows this request always amazes me: "As we forgive our debtors." It is really part of the entreaty for our own forgiveness. While we are asking for our own forgiveness we are also asking for the power to forgive others their debts against us. Jesus considered forgiving others an essential element to our prayer lives.

Jesus then directs us to pray for divine protection against temptation and the evil one. This request for divine protection comes after the acknowledgment of being forgiven and the directive to forgive others. Though there is no doubt that we need divine protection from the evil one in every area of our life, it is especially true that the devil tempts us and takes advantage of us by means of unforgiveness.

The final lines of this magnificent prayer remind us of the power of God to ratify and answer everything we have brought to His attention.

I would urge every Christian believer to incorporate every element of this divine prayer into their daily lives. After all, Jesus said, "In this manner, therefore, pray."

The following stories are the stories of women who learned to pray this prayer from the heart and were thus able to feel the incredible release and healing that comes when you forgive.

Forgiving a Murderer

How can you possibly forgive someone who has callously taken the most precious person out of your life? In Lynn's case the loss was even deeper and greater. The man who took the lives of those most dear to Lynn was unremorseful and belligerent. No platitude or formula could ease the suffering and pain Lynn felt. The torment continued for years. Lynn realized that redirecting her life into a healthy course would necessitate forgiving the man who destroyed her family.

The 1980s in America seemed to be the time of innocence and fun. Woman began to exercise to punchy tunes in colorful outfits with stylish ponytails. *Little House on the Prairie* was one of the most popular shows on television. Ronald Reagan was president and everyone felt like things were only going to get better.

That was exactly how Lynn felt. She never expected tragedy to strike in an era of such prosperity.

Lynn and her husband Richard had three handsome sons all attending the same college. The pride they took in all of their sons only escalated at their eldest son's announcement that he was engaged!

Richard and Lynn made plans to meet the bride-to-be the weekend of the college's homecoming game. After making the trek to the boys' college and settling into their motel room, Lynn and her friend Fay went shopping while Richard went to fetch the boys and their dates. Richard had opted to drive the boys that weekend because of the raucous element of the school parties.

When Lynn returned to her motel room, she flipped the television on while she prepared the food for the evening's celebration. As she busied herself pulling the groceries out of the market bags, the program was interrupted for an important news bulletin. Several college students from her boys' college had been involved in a car accident. The wreck claimed three lives. There were only two survivors. Lynn inched closer to the television. Perhaps it was someone she knew. Her breath caught in her throat as she recognized the crunched wreckage on the screen.

Within minutes, Lynn and her friend Fay were escorted to the hospital. Fay's daughter and two of Lynn's sons were among those pronounced dead at the scene. Lynn was informed that her oldest son and husband were in critical condition, barely hanging onto life. She spent the next several days at their bedside hoping and praying for their recovery. She wasn't even sure how to pray because the chances for their recovery were doubtful. During this time, Lynn had to make funeral arrangements for her two sons who had been killed. She also made plans to have her surviving son and husband flown by med flight to their hometown.

Once back at home, Lynn spent the next ten days at the hospital with her eldest son, Michael, and her husband, Richard. Michael succumbed to his injuries during that time and died. Then, only a day before Thanksgiving, the hospital asked Lynn to consider taking Richard off life support.

Lynn's pastor and a few friends showed up at the hospital. They could see that Lynn was in no shape to make such a critical decision. They urged her to go home and rest. Richard died that evening while still connected to life support.

All four funerals were held together. The service was both tender and uplifting. The church gathered around Lynn and sought to comfort and bless her in every way. However, nothing could prepare Lynn for life in the cavernous house she once shared with three rambunctious boys and her doting husband. She had no family. All the hopes and dreams she had shared with her husband and invested in her boys were suddenly gone in one great wave of tragedy. She was left to sort out, give away, and discard all that had once been the emblems of her happy family.

Lynn questioned the reason for such a painful calamity. Was God chastening her? Was this payback for some secret sin she had committed? She couldn't think of anything she had ever done to deserve such devastation.

Lynn's troubles were not over. The wounds that were trying to heal were torn open when the families of her sons' girlfriends filed wrongful death suits against Lynn. As Lynn struggled to repay a mountain of debt left by her husband and sons' medical bills, she was immersed in legal fees, defending herself against grieving parents—parents who Lynn had hugged and cried with at the hospital when they received the tragic news.

The man responsible for the accident was arrested, but the charges were dismissed when he agreed to go to rehabilitation. Lynn was angry! She and the other families had received a life sentence of loss and he got off with going to a facility that would help him with his alcoholism. Lynn tried to push the injustice of it all out of her mind. She knew her survival depended on it.

Lynn did write out a long list of questions for God, all beginning with "Why" or "What if?" She filed them away to save until the day that she met the Lord face-to-face. For now, there weren't any answers.

After the man who caused the accident was released from rehabilitation, he somehow obtained Lynn's phone number. He began to harass her with calls. He blamed her for the accident and accused her of ruining his life. His life?

It was difficult for Lynn to think of this man as anything but a monster. She never thought of him as a human being who God loved and gave His only Son for. Then one night she began to think about the woman in the Bible who was a known sinner. Jesus said that her "sins were many," yet He forgave her. Was it possible that God wanted to forgive this drunk too?

It was the first time that Lynn ever considered that she might have to actually forgive the man that took the lives of her sons and husband.

Lynn moved to the East Coast and worked hard to continue to pay off the medical bills. She was completely alone and her health had been weakened by the tragedy. For many years her life consisted of no more than the routine of attending church, working, eating, sleeping, and working some more. She was overwhelmed with grief but still determined to repay every debt she owed.

The empty moments were the hardest for her. She decided to fill the crevices of time with Bible study. This led her to listen to worship music and prayer. As she grew spiritually she felt a nagging urgency from God that she needed to forgive the drunk who had caused the death of her family. Every time Lynn felt the Lord press it upon her heart she cried. "Lord, it just feels like You are asking too much of me," she prayed.

The drunk managed to get Lynn's new phone number and the harassing calls began again. During this time God continued to gently press Lynn to forgive. God's Spirit tugged on her heart to release her pain and agony by simply handing the drunk driver completely over to Him. At the same time, Lynn felt God removing the sting of bitterness she felt. Though Lynn would never forget her beloved sons and husband, her memories of those she loved became tender and no longer shrouded by the unjust way they'd died.

Then it happened.

The drunk had called her yet again. Lynn clutched the receiver in her right hand. Before he could begin his tirade of accusations, Lynn said, "Because Jesus Christ has forgiven me, I choose to forgive you for what you did to my family." Silence.

Lynn waited. The line went dead. He had hung up. He never called Lynn again. She doesn't know what happened to that man. However, Lynn knows what God did in her that night. He completely healed her. The relief, comfort, and peace that had been absent from her life for months all came flooding back in. She was suddenly free to be the woman God had created her to be.

Though Lynn's ordeal is far from over, God has blessed her life over and over again. She has a new perspective. Lynn has learned that life is uncertain. Therefore Christians need to be prayed up, packed up, and ready to be picked up by Jesus every moment.

God led Lynn gently to the path of forgiveness and then urged her to take the first step. He supplied her with the will and power to forgive. Had Lynn not chosen to forgive the man who killed her family, she would have continued to be held hostage by his harassment and the damage he had caused. Instead, by God's grace and urging, Lynn chose to forgive. In forgiving the drunkard, she was set free from his harassment and able to seek out a new life with new joys and purpose.

Lynn had to forgive a man she barely knew but had brought devastation and unimaginable heartache to her life. Lynn never had to see her sons' killer again. However, our next story deals with a dear friend of mine who had to forgive the man who violated the covenant of marriage he made to her.

Forgiving Rejection

When a couple is married they take a vow to love and cherish, until death us do part. The violation of that covenant cuts deeply into the heart. The one who is unloved, uncherished, and forsaken is left with emotional outrage, deep insecurities, and a growing sense of vulnerability.

How do you begin to forgive someone who does not hold this sacred covenant precious? This was Donna's dilemma when her husband announced that he wanted to get a divorce after 15 years of marriage. His decision was final. He did not want to work at the relationship. He did not want to seek counseling. He wanted out.

Donna's first reaction was to sink into condemnation. She blamed herself. Maybe if she had worked harder at pleasing her husband. If only she had been a better mother. What could she have done to make the marriage work? It didn't ease her mind to recall her husband's constant criticism. He had called her a horrible wife and mother.

In reality, Donna had done everything she possibly could do to make the marriage work. When these condemning thoughts would rush into Donna's mind she learned to give them over to the Lord. She would pray, "Lord, please take these thoughts from me. I don't want to carry them around." The Lord comforted her with scripture: "Come to Me, all you who labor and are heavy laden, and I will give you rest" (Matthew 11:28). Because of the severity of the condemnation Donna battled, she sometimes had to pray this prayer and claim the promise of Matthew 11:28 every few minutes.

During this season of her life, Donna was told by a friend that those negative thoughts were like trash. They needed to be taken out to the curb and never brought back into the house. She had to make a conscious choice to take the rubbish running through her mind out to the curb. Within those garbage cans she surrendered not only her self-condemning thoughts, but also the bitter thoughts of anger and resentment toward her husband.

Donna chose to forgive her husband.

But even after the forgiveness, her mind often entertained thoughts about the future that she would never have, dreams that would never be realized, a family that was broken forever, and momentous future occasions she would experience alone. Donna discovered the gift of Jeremiah 29:11: "For I know the thoughts that I think toward you, says the LORD, thoughts of peace and not of evil, to give you a future and a hope." Donna replaced the thoughts of what would never be with thoughts of the good things God was planning for her.

Donna continued in her resolve to forgive her ex-husband by praying for him, counting her blessings, and living in the *now* of her life by focusing on Jesus. It's been three years since Donna's divorce, but Donna has never felt so free. She is completely healed from the hurt she once felt. Her ex-husband calls her every so often and still verbally assaults her; however, Donna is no longer compelled to retaliate. She is free from the pain of the past while he is still in bondage to it.

Like Donna, you might have to take specific measures to ensure that your resolve to forgive and be free continues. You too might need to imagine that every unforgiving thought is like rubbish on the floor of your house that needs to be swept up and dumped in the big bin outside. Remember: Trash is trash. If you keep those tormenting thoughts on the floor of your heart, they will clutter and take over your life. How much better to keep your heart clean by taking out the trash regularly!

Beginning Again

How do you forgive someone when you are bombarded daily by memories of bitter words, accusations, and hurtful actions? That was exactly the obstacle that Linda was facing. However, Linda had received assurances from God through His Word that He would bring blessings where the pain had once resided. Linda realized that if she ever hoped to step into the promises God had given to her, she would need to confront the issue of the unforgiveness she held in her heart. The wall of unforgiveness that she and her husband had erected between them threatened every possibility of God's promises.

Linda met Larry when they both worked at the same department store. Linda thought Larry was the most handsome man she had ever seen. Larry was kind to the young employee. Linda, because of her abusive upbringing, craved kindness. She fell deeply in love with Larry. He was ten years older, but the age difference only endeared him more to Linda.

Larry was very attracted to Linda. She had big blue eyes, long blonde hair, and an engaging personality. Plus, she was wild about him! There was only one thing standing in the way of a relationship between the two. Larry was a Christian and Linda was not. However, when Larry shared about the Lord with Linda, Linda made a commitment to Jesus. Larry even waited to make sure Linda's commitment was a sincere, personal decision and not one made because she wanted to please him or be in a relationship with him.

After three years of dating, Larry was sure. Larry and Linda were married. But if Linda expected marital bliss, she was dead wrong. She had entered the marriage with lots of emotional baggage from her parents' broken marriage. She had been raised without any affection. Her grandmother had verbally abused her and her brother had molested her.

Linda was looking for Larry to be her savior. He was not.

Friction soon began to build between the two of them. Linda sought the Lord in earnest, but as she drew closer to Jesus, the distance between her and Larry was more evident. Linda prayed for answers and help for her marriage, and she received promises from the Bible. She claimed these promises, stood on these promises, and prayed with these promises in mind.

Larry became even more distant and cold. When they tried to discuss what was going on between them, yelling ensued. Larry blamed Linda for everything that was wrong in the marriage. Linda accused Larry of never loving her. The conflicts were buried after fights, only to surface again later with greater ferocity.

Linda began to hate Larry. She could tell the feelings were mutual. Still she held on to what began to appear like hollow promises. At times Linda resolved that she would change Larry. However, no effort on Linda's part—good or bad—effected any change in Larry.

One day the fighting turned violent. Trapped in the confines of their small bathroom the arguing had begun. Suddenly Larry pushed Linda and she fell backward. Then he blocked the door. He turned and with all the pent-up anger in him he punched a hole through the wall right where her head had been. Linda was unsure of what would come next. Instead of more violence, Larry hung his head and said, "We can't go on like this." The words carried a finality that terrified Linda, and yet she knew they were true.

She left for a women's weekend retreat the next day. She cried through every study. The theme of the retreat was "Standing on the Promises of God." Every reference to God's promises rocked Linda.

"What had happened to God's promises?" She had a file full of promises but not one had come to fruition. She spied the pastor's wife and asked if she could have a moment alone with her.

Linda poured out all the marital issues she and Larry had been going through during the past 13 years. The pastor's wife listened with patience. Finally, Linda pulled out her journal and shared the promises God had given her. "What am I supposed to do with these?" she asked.

"You need to hold on to them and keep believing." Then the pastor's wife prayed for Linda.

Linda went home unsure of how everything she experienced at the retreat would play out. Almost immediately, when she entered the door, the fighting started. Larry stormed out of the house and Linda picked up the phone to call a friend to complain. As she lifted the receiver she felt the Lord speak to her. "What is that going to do for you?" She hung up.

She paused and then picked up the receiver again to dial her friend a second time. And again, she heard the Lord speak. "I asked you, what is that going to do for you?" Linda slammed the phone down. In that moment she realized that all her efforts over the last 13 years had done nothing to change Larry or improve her marriage. Linda prostrated herself on the cold tile of her kitchen floor. "You win, Lord. I have nothing left to fight with. I have no emotion, no strength, and no answers. There is no one else to turn to. There is nothing left. I don't know what needs to change, Lord, but You do." It came to Linda right in that moment: She needed to forgive Larry. It seemed so simple. The pain and injury they had inflicted on each other came to her mind and she forgave each offense.

Larry came home quite a while later. He stood just feet from her. Neither of them spoke for some time. Then Larry looked at her and said, "Is it over?" And she immediately realized that he was not talking about the relationship, but about the tensions and lack of forgiveness between them.

How he knew something had changed, she'll never understand. But she looked at him, and for the first time in years she loved him, really loved him. "Yes," she said. "It's all over."

Larry and Linda never discussed again who did what. The blame and accusations of the last years were simply gone. God had taken them away.

Things began to change rapidly from that moment on. There was a renewed love and partnership between the couple. After a year or so, both Larry and Linda got involved in their church. Larry took over a ministry that needed a new leader. Linda stepped in beside him to help. Today they happily serve together.

Linda and Larry both made the choice to forgive. When they did, God was able to bless their marriage and bring them into all the promises and purposes He planned for them.

Forgiving Stolen Innocence

One in five young girls will be sexually violated by someone they trust. The damage is deepened by both the loss of innocence and the desecration of trust. Those who were entrusted with protecting and valuing innocence instead chose to take advantage of that sacred trust to satisfy their own selfish and immoral cravings. Many women who were victims of such a violation when they were young remain hostages of unforgiveness.

I've talked to countless women who struggle to release the shame and humiliation of being molested. It is not an easy choice to forgive a molester. And women hesitate to do so because they are afraid it would empower the perpetrator or let him off the hook. However, those who chose to forgive found the opposite result to be true. Rather than empowering the perpetrator, it took the power to continue to hurt away from the offender. They were left healed and free to live in the good plans and purposes God had for them.

Betty was only seven when her parents' marriage disintegrated. Betty's mother was forced to work a series of odd jobs in order to provide for Betty and her brother. Her mother tended tables at restaurants during the day, served drinks at bars at night, and worked at nightclubs. Betty was left in the care and keeping of her ten-year-old brother.

Betty's home was devoid of God. They never went to church. There was no moral or righteous standard ever set by others. So at age seven, Betty had no understanding of what was right or wrong. She had a simple trust in her mother and brother and did whatever they told her to do.

Betty's mother's absence in the home had terrible consequences for Betty. Her brother, who had become a parental figure to her and her only source of love and companionship, stepped out of his protective role into a dark, corrupt, and evil role—that of molester.

Betty's once pure surrender to her mother and brother were lost. Her brother molested her daily, and she remained in the home because she didn't know any better. She complied in order to stay out of trouble. Somewhere back in the recesses of her mind she knew that if her mother ever found out, all hell would break loose. So Betty closed her eyes and just let it happen. The molestation continued until Betty finally moved to her dad's house.

Free from her brother, Betty tried to push it out of her mind. For years she thought she had successfully forgotten it. However, even as a teenager, Betty struggled with deep depression. In her late teens, as Betty watched a popular talk show dealing with family issues the subject of molestation was addressed. Out of nowhere, Betty suddenly felt the deep pain of her own defilement. She fell to her knees and began to scream to the empty room, "My brother molested me! My brother molested me!" She was in shock.

Though Betty tried to move on with her life, depression plagued her every step. She attempted to come to terms with her past or to dismiss it, but it kept intruding into her thoughts. These horrible memories and truths became too painful for her to bear. When

Betty turned 23, the wounds of the molestation resurfaced as her perspective on right and wrong became clear.

She decided to confront her brother. She felt she needed to ask him why he had taken advantage of her and destroyed her innocence. She arranged to have lunch with her brother, and when they met, Betty brought up the subject and demanded answers to her questions. He stumbled nervously through the lunch, making excuses for what he had done. Ultimately, he tried to justify his actions by saying, "Mom wasn't there to teach me any better." He treated it like it was not a big deal and accused Betty of wasting his time.

Betty left the lunch feeling empty and frustrated. She wanted him to apologize and beg for her forgiveness. He didn't. He wouldn't. Over time, Betty's anger grew. She determined she would never forgive him for what he had done or for his callous indifference toward his crime. Betty would hold him captive to the judgment he deserved.

Not long after this conviction to not forgive, Betty became a Christian and grew in her knowledge of God and His Word. In time, she began to hear the Lord speak to her heart about her brother and her childhood. When God would stir her heart with the concept of forgiveness she would immediately respond, "No way, God! Not him! Never!"

But God was gentle with Betty. He allowed her time to heal. Every few years, Betty again would feel the gentle, merciful prodding of God to forgive. Then she received news that her brother was having terrible struggles in life. His wife and daughter had left him. He had lost his impressive job. He was homeless and living on the streets.

Betty was taken aback by her emotions. She actually pitied her brother. She wondered how he felt and wondered if his guilt over what he did had undermined his success in life.

For the first time, Betty seriously considered forgiving him. God guided her to read 2 Corinthians 2:5-8, "But if anyone has caused grief, he has not grieved me, but all of you to some extent—not to be too severe. This punishment which was inflicted by the majority is sufficient for such a man, so that, on the contrary, you ought rather to forgive and comfort him, lest perhaps such a one be swallowed up with too much sorrow. Therefore I urge you to reaffirm your love to him."

This scripture did a number on Betty's heart. Her once angry heart now broke. She felt the Spirit of God fill her with love, mercy, and forgiveness for her brother. At that moment Betty made the choice to forgive her brother.

Betty has seen her brother only once since that time. He acted like nothing had ever happened, and this time it didn't bother Betty. Betty actually enjoyed spending time with her brother. The atmosphere between them was healthy, like it should be between a brother and sister. The best part of Betty's story is that her brother is now a Christian and on fire for Jesus. The Lord continues to restore the relationship that was severed between them because of sin and defilement.

If God hadn't continued to press Betty to forgive, Betty would still be filled with hatred, bitterness, and wrath toward her brother. Today, Betty is free, joyful, and unburdened by the injury of her childhood innocence. Not every story ends like Betty's. Not every woman feels the necessity to face her perpetrator. Sometimes forgiveness works best when you never see the perpetrator again. The choice to forgive is worked out uniquely in a myriad of ways in every life. Each story of forgiveness follows a different pattern to the great objective of freedom and joy.

Your Story of Forgiveness

The women in these stories all testify to the wonderful release they experienced when they chose to forgive. Their stories would have ended in brokenness, and tragedy had they not yielded to the gentle prodding of God to forgive. However, when they chose to forgive, their story became an epic tale of victory, joy, and healing. God wants to turn the story of your life into an epic adventure with a glorious ending. Your story doesn't have to end in bitterness, heartbreak, and loss. God is able to give you "beauty for ashes, the oil of joy for mourning, [and] the garment of praise for the spirit of heaviness" (Isaiah 61:3).

You can make the choice to forgive. No matter what has been done to you, you can forgive because Jesus has forgiven you. It all begins with the simple prayer that Jesus told us to pray: "Forgive us our debts, as we forgive our debtors." The freedom, the joy, and the promises of God are waiting for you on the pathway of forgiveness.

Questions for Study and Personal Reflection

1. Read 2 Corinthians 2:5-8. How do these verses minister to you about forgiveness?

2. Is there someone you need to forgive?

3. List any obstacles that stand in the way of forgiveness.

4. Write down any thoughts you need to gather and take out to the rubbish bin. (Once you write them down, release them to the garbage can by crossing them out one by one!)

5. What gentle urgings have you felt or heard from God concerning forgiving those who have injured you?

6. What testimony from this chapter ministered to you the most? Why?

Prayer

Dear Lord,

You were able to help Lynn, Donna, Linda, and Betty to forgive. I know that You can help me to forgive. I want the freedom that comes with turning over the transgressions of others to Your control and judgment. I also want to feel the freedom of being forgiven. Lord, release me from the agonizing burden of past hurts.

Help me to hear Your gentle urgings to forgive. Take my hand and lead me in Your pathway of grace. Let me feel Your presence and tenderness in this new venture. In Jesus's name, amen.

Chapter 10

Forgiving the Church

An older woman I know loves to ask everyone she meets, "Do you go to church?" If the answer is affirmative, she then asks, "Where do you go to church?" This question has made quite a few people uneasy. She's gotten her fair share of stories from those she talks to about how they stopped attending church when they got hurt.

Is this you? Even if it is painful to explore the idea, it's time to forgive and give church another chance. Why? Because God wants to bless you by placing you in a community of believers that will strengthen your faith.

Your place in the church body is waiting for you. God wants to use you in His assembly to be a blessing to others. The apostle Peter says, "Not returning evil for evil or reviling for reviling, but on the contrary blessing, knowing that you were called to this, that you may inherit a blessing" (1 Peter 3:9). When you are unforgiving of the assembly of God's people, you end up robbing yourself of the opportunity to bless others and be blessed yourself.

What Is Church?

The Greek word translated as church is *ekklesia*. Its literal meaning is "to be called out to meet." During New Testament times this was a common word. It denoted a gathering of citizens called out of their homes to a public assembly.

The church is a gathering of citizens who have been "called out" of this world into the assembly of Jesus Christ. In considering this assembly, it is vital to remember that those who have been called are not perfect. Notice how Paul describes them in 1 Corinthians 1:26-29, "For you see your calling, brethren, that not many wise according to the flesh, not many mighty, not many noble, are called. But God has chosen the foolish things of the world to put to shame the wise, and God has chosen the weak things of the world to put to shame the things which are mighty; and the base things of the world and the things which are despised God has chosen, and the things which are not, to bring to nothing the things that are, that no flesh should glory in His presence."

Yes, it is a group of faulted human beings whom Jesus calls into His assembly. Peter describes it this way in 1 Peter 2:9-10: "But you are a chosen generation, a royal priesthood, a holy nation, His own special people, that you may proclaim the praises of Him who called you out of darkness into His marvelous light; who once were not a people but are now the people of God, who had not obtained mercy but now have obtained mercy."

People are called out of darkness and into God's community, not because of their merit or goodness but because of God's mercy. When they respond to God's call, God transforms them, assembles them together, and makes them His people. We become not just an assembly of people, but God's assembly of people. And you can be sure that we won't be a perfect group until we all meet together in heaven, but that's no reason to give up on the whole concept of church.

The Bible directs us to go to church. "Let us consider one another in order to stir up love and good works, not forsaking the assembling of ourselves together, as is the manner of some, but exhorting one another, and so much the more as you see the Day approaching" (Hebrews 10:24-25).

Unhealthy and Healthy Churches

Just because an assembly is called a church does not mean that they teach, believe, and walk in God's Word. Those are essential elements of a productive, edifying, and good church. Even in New Testament times there were churches that were not godly and healthy. That is why the apostle John wrote, "Beloved, do not believe every spirit, but test the spirits, whether they are of God; because many false prophets have gone out into the world" (1 John 4:1).

But even a good church will have its problems. In Revelation chapters 2 and 3, Jesus addressed seven different churches that He walked among and observed. He had commendations for some, corrections for most, rebukes for a majority, and strong warnings for a few. So too there are some churches that should be left, some churches that should be helped, and still others that should be encouraged.

A healthy church is good for you. God created and built the church and continues to protect it and bless it. The church is to be a sanctuary, a place of refuge from pain and hurt. It is to be a house of prayer, where someone can lift her life up to God and be lifted in prayer by other believers. The church is to be a place of fellowship, where believers can have a sense of belonging, mutual understanding, and encouragement. The church is to be a place where people can gain and grow in knowledge of God through the study of the Bible. The church is necessary "for the equipping of the saints for the work of the ministry, for the edifying of the body of Christ, till we all come to the unity of the faith and of the knowledge of the Son of God, to a perfect man, to the measure of the stature of the fullness of Christ; that we should no longer be children, tossed to and fro and carried about with every wind of doctrine" (Ephesians 4:12-14).

I have heard many stories of believers who have been hurt by someone in the church, church leadership, cliques in the church, or dogmas of the church. Some of the people I have spoken to harbor hostility and refuse to attend church. However, the stories in this chapter have to do with people who were hurt by the church and chose to forgive. Their stories and lives have a very different ending. Instead of choosing isolation and lingering hostility, they forgave.

Misjudged!

Bob and Clara attended Calvary Chapel Westminster, London, and were one of the greatest blessings in the church. I wanted to send them off to their next church with a note pinned to Bob's lapel (like I did with my daughter when she went to kindergarten) explaining what a great blessing he and his family were.

Bob and Clara found a church in the area with great associations with other churches. With enthusiasm they and their children, 12 and 14 years old, took their seats in the main sanctuary and awaited the morning message. Before the service began, Clara felt a tap on her shoulder. One of the ushers informed her that her children were not permitted in the main assembly. Clara tried to explain that it was their first time and their kids were used to sitting with them. The usher dismissed her remonstrations and ordered her and the children out.

Bob wrote a kind letter to the pastor asking for permission for their children to sit with them. It was denied. But they were undeterred. They told their kids that they needed to go to class. Again Bob and Clara took their seats in the main sanctuary. The kids hated their class that was more about juvenile games than Bible study.

Bob decided to write another letter to the pastor. He outlined the situation and again requested that his kids be allowed to sit in church with him and his wife. In response, he received a formal reply that emphatically refused his request. There was no reason given other than "because the pastor said so." Bob called and asked for an appointment, thinking that maybe his letter was misunderstood. He was refused.

Bob and Clara were still not willing to give up. So they went again the following week. This time the pastor announced to the church that rather than studying the Bible on Sunday mornings they would be studying a book on church growth together as a congregation.

This notion did not sit well with Bob. He wrote another letter. He sent a copy of the letter to my husband, Brian. Brian thought the letter was gracious and presented Bob's argument in an intelligent, clear, and gentle way.

Bob received a response from the pastor informing Bob that he and his wife were no longer welcome at the church. Should they ever try to return, steps would be taken to expel them. Bob was shocked. He and his wife had never been asked to leave any place! And it wasn't a secular organization or an ungodly administration that was rejecting them—it was the church!

Bob and Clara chose to forgive because they realized that not every church was the same. Though the rejection stung, they realized the church was not a good fit for their family. They looked and found another church that welcomed them with open arms. Bob has served for quite a few years on the board and Clara has hosted many of the women's Bible studies.

What if Bob and Clara had given up on the church as a whole? They would never have looked for or found another church where they could be blessed and serve. They have no regrets about forgiving the church.

Maligned!

If anyone I know had a great cause to give up on the church, it had to be Audrey. She was young and vulnerable when she first met the exultant group of young people that comprised a new church in her town.

Audrey was emerging from a bad situation and still hurting from the events she had gone through. At her previous church an elder had raped her dear friend. Audrey went to the police with her friend when she filed charges. The elder in question happened to be the pastor's brother. He denied everything. Then the whole assembly became incensed at Audrey and accused the victim of lying. Audrey was no longer welcome at the fellowship, even after the charges proved to be true.

No doubt it was this painful tragedy that made Audrey so excited about the invitation to attend a new Bible study. Finding out that these young people met together, Bibles in hand, in a house, not a church building, made Audrey feel even safer.

In the beginning she loved the fellowship. She loved the teaching of the Word and felt that she was growing in her understanding of Jesus. One of the women in the fellowship offered to take Audrey in. Audrey was ecstatic. However, soon after Audrey moved into the house, problems began. The pastor, a single young man, was attracted to Audrey and told her so. That might not have been an issue if Audrey's new roommate hadn't been attracted to the pastor.

When the roommate discovered that the pastor had asked Audrey out, she went ballistic. From that time forward Audrey couldn't do anything right. Everything Audrey did was scrutinized and maligned. If Audrey helped with worship, she was grandstanding. If she talked to any of the young men, she was flirting. If she cried, she was full of self-pity. When she prayed and studied her Bible she was accused of playing the hypocrite.

Audrey tried to make things right. She apologized. She tried to serve harder. She volunteered to move out or go to a different church. "No!" she was reprimanded. She was to remain in the fellowship and submit to the leadership.

About this same time, Audrey caught the attention of Joe, another leader in the church. He was a godly man who helped the young adults mature in their faith. Audrey began to confide in him. Over time and lengthy conversations, Audrey realized that she was in love with Joe. He was everything that she had ever prayed for in a husband and more. The feelings were mutual. Joe wanted to ask Audrey to marry him.

Joe sought the approval of the church leadership to marry. Audrey's roommate, along with the pastor and a few others, were present when Joe presented his request. The roommate screamed, "You can't marry her. She is not worthy of you!" Then using her hands to demonstrate her point, the roommate raised one hand high in the air while reaching as far to the ground as possible with her other hand. "You are here," she said dramatically, looking at the raised hand. "And Audrey is here." Her eyes fell on the hand closest to the floor.

The pastor simply nodded. After all, this was the girl who had rebuffed his affections.

"I see," Joe said. And he did see! That evening Joe took Audrey to the beach. He felt it only fair to tell her the accusations that were raised against her. Audrey cried. "I don't know what else to do. I've tried everything. I've apologized. I've done everything they told me to do. There's nothing left."

Joe took Audrey's hand. "You could forgive them."

Forgive them? Up to this point Audrey considered the whole ordeal to be her fault. Suddenly she realized that she was not to blame. With a new perspective she realized the forgiving needed to be from her, and she knew it wouldn't be easy.

Holding hands, Joe and Audrey prayed together. Audrey made the conscious choice in prayer to forgive her roommate, the pastor, and all those who had made her feel so awful. When she opened her eyes, she smiled at Joe. Joe wasn't smiling. He looked very serious.

Audrey studied his face, concern etched in his forehead. Then she looked at his open hand. There in a box was a glittering ring. "Will you marry me?" Joe asked. Audrey practically grabbed the ring out of his hand as she exclaimed, "Yes! Oh yes…yes, I will!"

Joe and Audrey were married shortly after and decided to attend another church that had a great married couples study. They hadn't been attending very long when Audrey received a fateful call from her old roommate.

No sooner had Audrey said hello than a rush of familiar

accusations came pouring through the receiver. "Where have you been? You need to return and answer the charges against you." The roommate spewed one hateful thing after another.

Very calmly, Audrey said, "You and I both know that those charges are unfounded. The person who accused me called me last week and asked forgiveness. I forgave her just as I have already forgiven you."

The roommate began to cry. The accusation changed direction. "Why didn't you stop me?" she asked. "You should have rebuked me."

Audrey responded, "I prayed instead. I knew God could get through to you and I couldn't. God is trying to get through to you right now. And I forgive you."

Audrey hung up the phone. Yes, she had forgiven the church. And she had to make a conscious choice to forgive the others all over again. As she did this, there was no immediate release. Audrey found that she had to work through it choosing to forgive all over again every time she thought about any of it. Her resolve to forgive held strong.

Rather than stalemate in unforgiveness, Audrey was able to grow into a more gracious woman by the experience. She has a wonderful ministry to young women and is able to share deep insight into their struggles and issues as well as the love, grace, and forgiveness of Jesus.

It's never easy to be maligned, scrutinized, and misjudged. However, it seems to hurt worse when it comes from people who are supposed to be operating in grace and representing Jesus. Audrey's full release came when she was finally able to separate her roommate's attitude from Jesus's heart toward her.

If you are struggling with someone in the church who has maligned your character, you must separate their actions from Jesus. A great way to do this is to reread the Gospels noting Jesus's great tenderness with people. I especially love the story of the woman at the well in John 4 as well as the story of the woman caught in adultery in John 8. These women were full-fledged sinners, yet the Lord was kind and gracious toward them. He offered those women hope and did not condemn them.

The Fallout of Burnout

There was a time when I collapsed in tears on our back porch. All I could seem to say was, "Jack of all trades, and master of none." That's exactly how I felt too. I was doing a hundred things in the church and at home and feeling totally ineffective in every area of my life.

Have you experienced this meltdown? At the crux of such a burnout is the burden of feeling overly responsible for the people and duties in the church. I think that is how Martha felt. Her story is recorded in Luke 10. While Martha bustled around making preparations for housing Jesus, her sister Mary simply sat at Jesus's feet and listened to Him. Martha grew more and more agitated as she thought about Mary enjoying Jesus's company while she had to do all the work. After brooding about it for a while, Martha told Jesus about her feelings. It was no longer just Mary's fault, but it was also Jesus's for allowing Mary to sit at His feet while Martha slaved alone. You can sense this accusation in her address to Jesus, "Lord, do You not care?" That transference of anger is exactly what happens in the church.

Unforgiveness toward the church might begin with feeling overly burdened with responsibility. Accompanying this feeling is a sense of isolation. No one else is helping or feels as committed to the responsibilities of the church. When you are expending all your energies and working alone it is easy to get the Martha Complex.

I have wondered if her thought process went something like this: "Here I am working all alone doing the dishes, cleaning the kitchen, kneading the bread, and preparing the lamb while Mary sits at Jesus's feet. She should be in here helping me. I would love to sit at Jesus's feet, but who would do the cooking if I went in there?

Maybe if I clang the pots around loudly enough, she will get the hint and come in here. Hmm. Maybe I'll clang them louder and then add a few loud sighs. What? She is still just sitting there. Why does Jesus just let her sit there? He must know that I am alone in here doing all the work. Why doesn't He tell her to come help me? Maybe He loves her more. Maybe He doesn't care about me."

Resentment often accompanies burnout. It did with Martha. Her sense of burnout made her upset with Jesus. The same thing happens in the church. People who are undervalued, overworked, and isolated often become resentful of the body of Jesus—the church.

That's what happened with my friend Brenda. At first she was ecstatic to be part of all the church activities. She loved feeling like a contributor to the welfare of the church.

She became extremely close to the pastor's wife, Patty, who began to lean on her for various tasks and services. Brenda threw all her creativity, energy, and time into doing whatever the pastor's wife asked. Often Brenda neglected her family to help Patty.

Eventually Patty drew Brenda into her confidences. She gossiped about other members and warned Brenda against associating with them. This made Brenda feel even more pressure to help the pastor's wife in whatever she needed. As Brenda continued to push herself she noticed that nothing pleased Patty. Brenda tried harder, but her efforts were never enough.

Soon Brenda was exhausted. She found herself completely ostracized by Patty when she expressed her need for a break. The calls from the church secretary to do work continued, but Patty refused to acknowledge Brenda's presence, even when they were in the same room.

When Brenda's resentment built up in her heart, she resigned from every ministry and quit going to church altogether. Not long after, she received a letter in the mail from the women's board. In it the pastor's wife had outlined Brenda's failings and shortcomings.

Brenda wasn't just mad at the pastor's wife—now she was mad at the church! It was the church that had left her to work alone. It was the church that was snubbing her. It was the church that was demanding so much of her time. It was the church that was pointing out all her shortcomings.

A few months later, Dave, Brenda's husband, received a job transfer across the state. It wasn't long before Dave found a new church. He couldn't wait for his family to attend with him. Sunday after Sunday passed, but Brenda still wasn't ready to go to church. She held all churches responsible for Patty's actions. She wasn't sure she could trust a church anymore.

Every Sunday, Dave and the kids asked Brenda to join them. Finally, Brenda relented and chose to attend. The sermon message spoke to her and she loved the worship time. Oh, how she had missed church. Some women in the fellowship greeted her and invited her to join the weekly women's study. "No way!" Brenda thought. "Never again!" Though her heart ached for girlfriends that she could confide in, giggle with, and fellowship with, she refused to get involved.

One day Brenda woke up to the realization that she had been letting the pastor's wife hold her captive. Her loneliness was due to the fear that she would encounter another Patty at this church but in a different dress and face. Brenda poured out her fears to God in prayer.

With trepidation, Brenda began to take an active role in the women's ministry at her new church. She became particularly close to an older godly woman in the fellowship. The woman encouraged Brenda to go to a retreat with her. In the quiet of their room on Friday evening, Brenda, with tears flowing, told the woman everything. The woman listened with empathy. When Brenda finished, the woman asked, "But have you forgiven Patty and the church?"

"Forgive her?" she asked. Forgiveness was a concept Brenda had not even considered.

"Yes. Forgive." The woman explained the dangers of holding on to bitterness, grudges, and pain. "You need to forgive so you can be free to serve the Lord with joy again."

Brenda suddenly understood. That night she chose to forgive. It was not an easy choice. Brenda realized that like Martha, she had become overly concerned with too many things. She had blamed Jesus for Patty's indifference and unkindness. Brenda realized the importance of sitting at Jesus's feet and learning what He, and not others, wanted of her.

Since that time, Brenda has learned some important boundaries that allow her to spend time with Jesus and volunteer in select ministries.

When You're the Problem in the Church

Many people get the misguided notion that the church is too good for them. They are actually afraid of not being good enough to be around other good people. They resent the church because they are convinced the church is out to judge them or disqualify them. They are looking for an excuse to leave or to hold unforgiveness toward the church. That might have been the case with Tasha.

Unlike Brenda, Tasha was not treated badly by the pastor's wife. She *was* the pastor's wife! Tasha knew she had issues. You couldn't grow up with a background like hers and not exhibit some of the residual effects from time to time. Perhaps Tasha should have had more time to heal before she served beside her husband, or perhaps everything she endured was necessary to force her to grow.

To say that Tasha was misunderstood was an understatement. Tasha had an anger problem. She could flare up over trivial things. She often vented her anger on the hapless person who was standing closest to her.

Anger was not Tasha's only issue. She also dealt with frequent episodes of depression. She would withdraw, refuse to talk, or become sullen when one of the episodes came on her.

Even as Tasha struggled with her inner battles, she was growing spiritually. She read her Bible voraciously. God gave her stirring

Bible studies that she delivered to the women under her care. She was passionate about God and a born evangelist.

The other women in leadership didn't know what to do with Tasha. How could she be both so dynamic and so troubled? They sent their husbands to talk to her husband, Steve. Steve knew that Tasha had problems, but he could see so much growth in her. He dearly loved his wife. He wanted to protect her and provide her with an atmosphere where she could spiritually prosper.

Many of Tasha's issues stemmed from a deep distrust of people. She was learning to fully trust and entrust to God. Steve feared that any confrontation would set Tasha back.

The other leaders didn't see it that way. They planned an intervention. They brought Tasha into a room and one by one shared their concerns about her behavior. Just as Steve thought, Tasha was crushed. The intervention accentuated all the feelings of distrust that Tasha was dealing with. Tasha became even angrier.

Intervention, confrontation, counseling, and everything else they could think of were attempted by the leadership. Tasha resented it all. She found it hard to work alongside those who had confronted her. Especially now that she knew how they really felt about her.

Tasha was miserable. She hated her temper as much as anyone else. Her depression terrorized her. She wanted to be happy like other believers. She began to pray. As much as she didn't want to acknowledge it, the essence of what the leadership was saying was right. Maybe they didn't do it the right way, but they were trying to help her. In that moment she chose to forgive them. When she forgave, she felt freer than she had in months.

Tasha began to deal with her anger and depression. She presented them to the Lord and asked for His help. She began to discover other areas of hidden hostility in her heart. She made a habit of confessing each one and choosing to forgive each offense that came to mind.

Tasha's anger soon subsided. The depression began ebbing too. She realized that forgiveness was the key to her newfound freedom.

Talking to Tasha now, one would never know that she once suffered from severe fits of anger and depression. It's hard to imagine she could be anyone other than the joyful woman she is today.

Don't Get Ripped Off

Maybe you've had a bad church experience. Don't let that experience rob you from the blessing of the church community. Jesus wants you to be a part of His great big church. If you've had a bad experience with the church, here are seven ways you can move forward.

1. Recognize the source of the problem, whether it be a person or a situation.
2. Choose to forgive the individuals who have harmed you.
3. Find a church that is a good fit.
4. Set healthy boundaries when it comes to volunteer work.
5. Be willing to acknowledge your contributions to the issues.
6. Pray for your pastor and other church leaders.
7. Pray for the members of your church.

We cannot control how others in the church behave, but we can pray that we ourselves would be more like Jesus. We can use their actions to propel us to draw closer to Jesus and minister His grace to others.

In some cases the Lord might call you to stay, work through, and pray for the situation in the church. Other times the Lord might call you to attend a different fellowship where the leadership is more in tune with the gospel. Whatever the case, the important issue is to not blame the church for those who have hurt you. Remember, the church is Jesus's creation.

When you choose to forgive those in the church who have hurt you, you set yourself free to be available to minister wherever God chooses to place you.

Questions for Study and Personal Reflection

1. Use 1 Corinthians 6:9-11 to remark on the condition of those who are in the church.

2. Read 1 Corinthians 1:26-28 and comment on those God has chosen.

3. From 1 Peter 2:9-10 describe the transformed condition of the church.

4. What does the passage from 1 Peter minister to you about the people that are in your church?

5. How do you think a biblical perspective on church members will help you to "forgive" the church?

6. Reflect on the attributes of church leadership from 1 Timothy 3:1-7.

7. Write a personal prayer for the leadership in your church.

Prayer

Dear Lord,

You are gracious and kind and forgiving. It is so hard when people in the church and in church leadership don't act like You. I admit that I have been angry with Your church. Please forgive me so I can forgive others. I know You love those in Your church even as You love me in all my imperfections. Help me to forgive and love Your children. Lead me and make me a blessing to Your church on earth. In Jesus's name, amen.

Chapter 11

The Power of an Apology

I had forgotten about the incident. Honestly, I had chosen to forgive it just hours after I heard about it. Somebody I cared about and considered a friend had said something demeaning about me. It had gotten back to me.

Just a few days later, I ran into him at the store. We had a short, friendly conversation. As I was exiting the door I added, "Hey, Vince, why did you tell Nathan that I shot my mouth off to Jane?" Then I left; I never saw his reaction.

My friend, Vince, made a beeline for my husband, Brian's, office. He apologized profusely for what he had said and asked Brian to let me know how sorry he was. Brian did, and I let the whole thing go.

Two years later, I was attending a funeral when I saw Vince. We had a wonderful conversation together as we recalled childhood memories that we shared. As the conversation ebbed, Vince paused. "Listen," he said, his tone suddenly turning serious. "I want to say I'm sorry about ever saying that you shot off your mouth."

"I put that away a long time ago," I answered sincerely.

Vince was unmoved. "Nevertheless, I just wanted to say I am really sorry." Then he left.

I stared after him. Something powerful had just taken place. Yes, I had forgiven him a long time ago. No, I didn't hold anything against him. Yet the apology stirred something deep and tender in my heart. I loved him all the more for it. He, a civic leader and a successful businessman, had humbled himself. He had admitted he was wrong about what he had said. He had apologized for the sentiments he had expressed. He had done it sincerely. It was truly amazing!

His apology got me thinking about the power of an apology. In the other chapters we have concentrated on the role of the person who is in the right and has been violated. But what about the person who is in the wrong?

Apologizing seems to be losing momentum in our society. Most people pride themselves on being right. When they are caught in the wrong, they justify, excuse, deny, or blame someone else for what they did!

Those who postpone forgiveness until they get an apology never get the opportunity to forgive. They are left holding a bag of gnawing resentment.

Having to Say You're Sorry

He absolutely, downright refused! He would not apologize. He tightened his lips lest the fateful words slip out. No amount of cajoling from his mother or father would make him apologize. When his lips began to loosen, his parents were hopeful. No apology was forthcoming. Instead Warren screamed, ranted, and raved at the injustices of life for over an hour. Though Warren was only three at the time, he had already acquired the demeanor of most adults.

Why is it so difficult to utter the words, "I was wrong"? Most days it's not that hard, especially if you're really in the right. But a sincere apology requires the admittance that you are at fault and have the capacity to not get it right.

You might ask yourself, "Why is it so hard to come to terms with my shortcomings?" I think the answer is that once we realize we are fallible, we begin to doubt our ability to ever be right. We take getting it wrong way too seriously, as if once we have been discovered to be in the wrong, we will never get it right.

Getting it right, though, is the greater exception. Most of the time, we get it wrong. Once we realize that we are not infallible, we are ready to start a wonderful new pattern of saying we are sorry and meaning it.

Another aid to opening us up to the blissful habit of apologizing is the recognition that everyone gets it wrong sometimes. We are not alone in our folly. King Solomon once said, "For there is no one who does not sin" (2 Chronicles 6:36). Again, to quote Alexander Pope, "To err is human." Everyone gets it wrong sometimes.

One of the greatest aspects of motherhood is the humility it brings. Often the mistakes I made raising my children are the fodder of family laughter. The laughter is not at my expense but with my endorsement. I am so relieved that they have chosen to laugh at my folly, accept my profound apologies, and walk in forgiveness toward their mother. Whew!

What else lurks at the base of our unwillingness to apologize? Often it can be fear. What will happen to me if I admit I was wrong? Will it be used against me? Will I be ostracized?

Sure, there are some people who take apologies as the opportunity to upbraid someone and feel superior, but that is their problem. We don't want to miss the incredible release an apology can bring just because of a few cranks!

The greatest reason that we are loath to say "I am sorry" is pride. I don't want anyone to think less of me. If others find out that I am wrong in this instance, will they ever trust me again? An over-preoccupation with the image we portray to others will keep us from apologizing.

Rather than an apology causing people to distrust you, a frank apology is more likely to cause people to trust you. If you can be that honest about your own failings, then certainly you will be honest in other areas.

Have you offended someone? Why don't you apologize? Once you apologize, the ball is in their court. If they refuse to forgive you, give them this book. If they choose to forgive you, you have successfully closed that painful chapter of your life.

An apology doesn't mean you have to be best friends with the person you offended. Nor does it mean that you have let them dominate your life. An apology does not give the offended the right to criticize you, demean you, or hold anything against you. It does give them the opportunity to forgive and let go.

Tammy's Story

In her job as a supervisor in a company, Tammy worked frequently with a particular woman. They got along well, but one day they had an uncharacteristic disagreement. The conflict between them escalated and harsh words were exchanged.

In her mind, Tammy justified her actions. Over and over she played out the scene, always portraying herself as both the victim and the heroine. Still, Tammy felt an ache in the pit of her stomach. She knew it would not be in the best interest of the company or her ongoing work relationship with this woman to allow the tension to remain. Besides, Tammy and her coworker were Christians, and she knew that they were not setting a great example for others.

Tammy wanted to make it right, but every time she remembered the unkind words, the anger would flood over her again and overrule all her intentions to make it right. She began to pray, asking God for help. It was several days before Tammy finally got an answer—but it wasn't the answer she wanted to hear. The Lord spoke to Tammy and told her to go and apologize to her coworker. God impressed on Tammy's heart to ask her coworker for forgiveness for the harsh things she had said.

Tammy waited for confirmation. An apology would not be an easy thing to offer. For the next week or so, every time Tammy opened her Bible, there before her eyes was a Scripture about love, forgiveness, and obedience. Tammy knew what she had to do. She swallowed her pride and called her coworker to set up a meeting. The woman agreed to get together.

The closer the meeting got, the more Tammy could feel her heart pounding. Walking into the room where they were to meet, Tammy could feel her hands grow clammy. Tammy had no idea how her coworker would respond. She only knew what she had to do.

The woman, seeing Tammy walk in, rose and stormed over toward her. Before the woman could say a word, Tammy impulsively wrapped her arms around her coworker. "Please forgive me; it was my fault. I don't want to lose your friendship or your respect. I am so sorry."

The woman melted in Tammy's arms. To this day, recalling that moment brings tears to Tammy's eyes. A beautiful friendship was initiated by her apology. The two women continued to work together, collaborating on many successful projects. Even now, years after they have both retired, the two women are close friends.

Tammy shared with me the valuable lesson she learned through that situation. "What the enemy means for harm, the Lord can turn and use for good, if we give it to Him. God waits until we are willing to take the first step before He helps us with the next step." When Tammy made the first step to obey God and apologize, He gave her the strength to carry through with her resolve.

Emma's Story

Cell phones are both a blessing and a curse. It's great to be able to stay in constant communication with those we love. It is also a blessing to be able to reach and be reached when needed. However, there are times when cell phones are just too handy.

That's what happened to Emma. Emma had taken Doug and Celia in and treated them like her own children. They dropped by her house. They ate dinner with her family. Doug's sister, Suzie, was even best friends with Emma's own daughter, Rachel. Everything was going great until Emma heard that Doug was having a birthday party. Neither she nor her daughter had been invited.

Emma understood why she might not be invited. She was a mother figure in Doug's life, and this party was for young people. But what about Rachel? Why hadn't she been invited?

Without thinking, Emma picked up her cell phone and typed a raging text to Doug. It was totally out of character for Emma to do or say anything like this. Just minutes after she pushed the "send" button, she regretted what she wrote. She reread the text. "Ouch," she thought.

Doug didn't answer her. He didn't stop by either. A week went by and there was no word from Doug. Emma wrote Doug asking for a response. His only response was a distant, "I hope you are doing better." Emma was crushed. She expected more from the young man who had become like a son to her.

Emma called a friend and explained the situation. "I don't know what to do," she cried into the ever-ready cell phone.

"Yes, you do," her friend told her. "Why don't you try texting him an apology? Since this thing blew up over a text, I think a text would be a great way to make it right."

Emma did just that. She typed out a heartfelt apology to Doug. His response thrilled Emma's heart. Doug is back to dropping in at Emma's house. He's learning to show a little more sensitivity, and Emma has learned the power of an apology.

Debbie's Story

Debbie shudders at the memory of the time she almost lost her best friend. It was petty, really. Debbie and Terry were best friends. Their kids played together. Their families shared meals together. The two women confided in each other both their joys and heartaches. But something changed when Terry and her husband started being used by the Lord. Instead of being happy for them, Debbie found herself being annoyed. Terry didn't have as much time for Debbie anymore.

Soon little things that Terry did or said began to annoy Debbie. She stopped wanting to be with Terry at all. Terry could sense Debbie's annoyance. Things between them got palpably uncomfortable. It grew so tense between them that for two months they didn't talk at all.

As much as Debbie tried to justify her feelings, she felt miserable. She knew she had sacrificed something very precious for no logical reason. Debbie began to pray and ask the Lord to remove the "yucky" feeling resident in her heart. As she prayed, the Lord spoke to her heart and said, "Debbie, humble yourself, call Terry, and ask for forgiveness for the way you've been acting."

Debbie was afraid. "Lord, if that's really You, give me the strength to call and apologize," she prayed. No sooner had Debbie said "Amen" than she felt an irresistible urgency to call Terry and make it right.

Debbie dialed her friend. As soon as Debbie heard Terry's greeting, she plunged in. "Terry, I am sorry for the way I've been behaving. Would you please forgive me? I love you so much and I am so sorry!"

Without hesitation, Terry practically shouted back into the phone, "I love you so much too!"

Debbie learned that forgiveness is an act of humility that only God can birth in us. Asking forgiveness involves dying to ourselves. It involves trusting God fully and putting your reputation into His hands.

Even as we need to make the choice to forgive, apologizing is also a choice. Once we make that choice, we need to pray and ask God for the strength to carry out that resolve. How people respond is up to them. Our admittance of wrong makes us right with our heavenly Father. He will work out all the other details.

Apologies Change Hearts

If anyone ever needed to apologize to someone, certainly it was Job's friends.

Job was an upright man. Satan, the adversary of God, hated him because God took pleasure in him. Satan tried to make Job's life so miserable he would curse God.

Though Satan assailed Job with the murder of his children, the loss of his wealth, and terrible physical suffering, Job refused to curse God. During Job's time of suffering, his friends came to comfort him. When they saw Job, they barely recognized him in his deep state of grief. They sat down beside him and wept. For seven days they were unable to speak. If only they had kept silent! Because when they finally began to speak, they blamed Job for his condition. They wrongly concluded that Job had secret sins God was punishing him for.

Job was so disheartened by his friends that he said, "Miserable comforters are you all!" (Job 16:2). If Job felt bad before they came, he felt worse in their presence. After enduring days of accusations, insinuations, and condemnation, God entered the conversation and defended His servant Job. However, the ordeal was not over. God required that Job's friends apologize to Job. They were required by God to give Job seven bulls and seven rams "lest I deal with you according to your folly; because you have not spoken of Me what is right, as My servant Job has" (Job 42:8).

God restored Job's losses only after Job prayed for his friends. In other words, Job was only restored after he accepted his friends' apology.

In Matthew 5:23-24, Jesus said, "If you bring your gift to the altar, and there remember that your brother has something against you, leave your gift there before the altar, and go your way. First be reconciled to your brother, and then come and offer your gift."

An apology can be a powerful thing. Refusing to apologize can interfere with our service to Jesus. Is there someone you need to say you are sorry to? Why not pray right now and ask God to give you the strength to humble yourself, go to them or write to them, and say you are sorry? You never know how God might use that apology powerfully in their life.

Back when Vince apologized to me, something moved so powerfully in me. I loved him more for it. My respect for him grew immensely. I could not resist forgiving him. When we step up and apologize to people we care about, we free ourselves from unforgiveness and allow the relationship to grow.

Questions for Study and Personal Reflection

1. Read Matthew 5:23-24 and summarize Jesus's instruction.

2. Matthew 7:12 says, "Therefore, whatever you want men to do to you, do also to them." With this in mind, write out the apology you would like to receive from someone who offended you.

3. What has kept you from apologizing?

4. Recall a time someone apologized to you. How did it make you feel? How did you respond?

5. Describe a time when you needed to apologize to someone else. Include your feelings at the time and what happened when you chose or didn't choose to apologize.

6. Someone once said, "Spiritual growth can be measured by the brevity of time between when you realize you were wrong and you apologize." Write a prayer asking God to help you to be more willing to admit wrong and apologize for it.

Prayer

Dear God,

Help me lean on You for strength as I trust Your leading when I need to apologize. Release me from a hardened heart and from pride, so I can step forward and ask for forgiveness when I need to and also extend forgiveness to someone seeking it. Show me the relationships in my life that would be enriched by the gift of an apology. And when I am reluctant, Lord, may I always remember Your forgiveness and how it has transformed me and my circumstances. Thank You, Jesus, for already accepting my apologies and forgiving me. In Jesus's name, amen.

Chapter 12

Ongoing Forgiveness

Making the choice to forgive is not a once-in-a-lifetime proposition. Every day affords many opportunities to exercise forgiveness. For example, each time I get in the car and drive anywhere, I am given plenty of chances to choose to forgive.

I forgive the guy who pulled out in front of me without warning me.
I forgive the person who is tailgating me.
I forgive the person who ran the red light.
I forgive the person who nearly sideswiped me.
I forgive all five people who wouldn't let me pull over.
I forgive the lady who honked at me when I was trying to merge.

The more we choose to forgive and not take offense, the easier it is to choose forgiveness the next time we encounter an opportunity. The more we exercise the act of forgiveness, the more freedom we will experience.

It takes less effort to extend forgiveness in some situations than in others. When I don't have to see the person who offended me on a regular basis, I cross over to forgiveness more readily. When boundaries or distance follow the decision to forgive, it can be easier to forgive both the offense and the offender. When I can see a genuine change in the person I forgave, the choice to forgive is reinforced. If, however, the person I chose to forgive lives close by and continues to act offensively, I am tempted to return to an attitude of unforgiveness.

The proximity and nature of the offender does not negate the need to choose to forgive. It does, however, intensify the need to pray and receive divine strength to forgive. No matter what the conditions are, holding on to unforgiveness is never the right choice. It will leave you in greater bondage to the offender and wreak havoc on your life.

Years ago I watched a young girl testify at a trial against the man who had assaulted and raped her. There were other young victims, but they refused to appear in court. The strong, bold testimony of this brave girl convinced the jury of the rapist's guilt and sent a dangerous criminal to jail. Later, when she was asked why she agreed to step forward, she said, "He was able to make one hour of my life miserable. I was determined not to give him any more time than he had already taken from me."

That girl got it right. She was unwilling to let the offender steal any more from her than he had already taken. She refused to let him have her joy, her quality of life, and any more of her thoughts. Even if your offender lives nearby, even in your home, by choosing to forgive, God can restore your joy, quality of life, and your thoughts. Forgiveness shifts the control over your life away from the offender and gives it to God.

The following are the stories of men and women who made the choice to forgive someone very close to them. They were challenged during the times when emotional or physical wounds were inflicted and they continue to be challenged every day to continue to choose forgiveness. They have decided to embrace forgiveness as an ongoing act. Their victory in Jesus is evident in their perseverance, their changed hearts, and their daily renewed commitment to be faithful forgivers.

A Difficult Dad

Betsy grew up walking on eggshells around her dad. His temper was legendary. Just about anything could set him off. He seemed to delight in berating his wife, his daughter, his sons, and anyone else who crossed him. With his cruel words and domineering personality, he could make even the strongest person shake in their boots.

Betsy found it easier to avoid him than to try to pacify him. His expectations for her were extremely high. As soon as she graduated from high school as an honor roll student, she got as far away from him as possible. Betsy ended up traveling all over the United States trying to find herself. It was the time of hippies, free love, and ready accommodations. Her travels landed her at a Christian farm community on the Pacific Coast. She met a group of Christians who led her to Jesus. It was everything Betsy had ever wanted.

Betsy remained at the community until her faith was fully established. Then she decided it was time to take the gospel back home to her parents and siblings. Betsy was not sure of the reception she would receive. She had left a house in turmoil.

Her homecoming was better than Betsy had anticipated. Her parents were overjoyed to see her safe and sound. They listened to her testimony with interest. While Betsy stayed with her parents, they watched her intently to see if her faith was genuine or not.

Days after Betsy moved back to the Pacific Coast, her father called her long distance to share some exciting news with her. Both her mother and father had asked Jesus into their hearts. They too had become Christians. Betsy's first reaction was immense joy.

Hours later, though, she had to come to terms with some feelings that she hadn't dealt with since she had gotten saved. She realized that she still resented her dad's fits of anger. Would things be different now that he was a Christian?

Betsy resolved to forgive him that day and put the past in the past.

After Betsy married, her parents moved to California to be near her. Betsy's father was definitely different, but every once in a while his old nature cropped up. Inevitably, every time they got together

her dad would end up saying something offensive. His attitude and words were still very hurtful.

Betsy realized she needed to forgive her dad again and again. She prayed for greater resolve and God blessed her with the ability to see her dad through His eyes. Though her dad is not completely transformed, someday, when he is in the presence of Jesus, he will be. Betsy was able to wipe her dad's slate clean.

Betsy's dad delights in being close to his daughter. Betsy still struggles at times, but having made the choice to forgive, she prays and resolves to keep walking in the path of victory. That victory allows her to maintain a loving relationship with her parents.

A Wayward Husband

Denise had to learn to practice forgiveness very early on in her marriage. Her husband, Nick, had promised that alcohol would not be a part of their lives together. However, six months after they were married, Nick's friend brought wine coolers to their house to celebrate. Denise overlooked the incident, thinking it would never happen again. She was wrong.

Nick soon began what is called a seasonal or cyclical alcoholic pattern. He would drink for a season then realize how it was affecting Denise and the kids and stop for a while. Then something would trigger this cycle and Nick would start drinking again. As time progressed, so did the frequency and intensity of these patterns. Each cycle was worse than the previous one.

Occasionally, Nick attended AA meetings and Denise sought out help from support groups. All the attendees, like Denise, were living with alcoholics. It helped Denise to know that she wasn't alone. It was there that she learned about detachment, which is a state of not judging or condemning a person, but separating oneself from the adverse effects another person's behaviors can have upon our lives. She was supposed to detach herself from the situation and the person drinking. They said this would keep her from feeling the adverse effects of Nick's drinking.

This concept appealed to Denise. However, she had noticed that many of the women in the group would talk about this concept and claim to have achieved it, and yet they exuded bitterness and anger. Denise wholeheartedly wanted to preserve her marriage and her joy. Ultimately, she realized that she needed God to work a miracle.

Denise began to pray. Though she didn't feel any immediate relief, she knew God would help her. Her struggle with Nick was not "how" she would forgive him, but "if" she could forgive him once more. She asked herself many times, "How could he? Why should I forgive him again? Why do I have to keep going through this?"

Denise found herself unwilling to ask God to help her to forgive Nick because she was sure God would give her the grace to forgive, and she didn't want to forgive him! Denise wanted to stay mad at Nick. He was ruining their lives!

One day, Nick was arrested for drunk driving. His choice to drink under the influence of alcohol had resulted in a man's death, and he was sentenced to time in jail. With Nick locked up and away from liquor, Denise had some personal time to heal.

For the first year of Nick's incarceration, he and Denise did not have any physical contact. All their communication was through glass windows, letters, and telephone calls. It was during this time that the difficult process of full disclosure began. Nick confessed that he had not been faithful to Denise.

In the past, Denise would've been outraged, but now, seeing Nick in his prison garb, she could only feel pity. She chose to forgive him.

After Nick had been in jail for over a year, they were allowed family visits. Denise was concerned about resuming physical contact with Nick. She wept when she held Nick's hand for the first time in a year. She grieved over the innocence and purity that had been lost between them. She chose again to forgive and prayed for the resolve to completely erase the mental tally of his transgressions.

Since that time, Nick has been released from prison and Denise's resolve continues to be tested. Though Nick stopped drinking and became a faithful husband, the painful memories continue to pop up at unexpected times. Denise has to make the conscious choice to forgive each time. God is helping Denise to remain vigilant over these thoughts and take them captive. For inspiration, she holds on to 1 Peter 4:8, "And above all things have fervent love for one another, for love will cover a multitude of sins."

Every day Denise has to make the conscious choice to forgive again. It's not an easy choice, but it is the only one that brings any continued hope of restoration and healing. Her marriage continues to heal.

The Landlord and the Lord

Don served as a missionary for many years in Eastern Europe. While planting a church in the village where he lived, he rented a facility from a man named Checu, who was also a fellow believer. However, relations became strained between the two men. Checu worried about his property and didn't trust the kids who were coming daily to the small fellowship. Many of them had come out of questionable backgrounds and still belonged to punk rock bands.

Checu and Don argued and parted ways. Later, Don was called back to the States to pastor a church. After a few years, he organized a mission trip with some of the men in his fellowship to return to Eastern Europe and help with a Christian conference during Holy Week.

During the first night of outreach, Don and his group noticed a group of young men exiting a building nearby. Don engaged them in conversation, and discovered that they had just had a time of Christian fellowship. Soon, the pastor of the young men's church joined the conversation. He invited Don and the guys from the

States to join them for their Easter morning service. Don and the men accepted.

They gathered with a large group in the upper room of a house. A large and very realistic tomb had been built and placed on the stage. The worship team assembled in front of the empty tomb and led the congregation in a moving time of praise. A dozen children entered from the rear of the room in costume and came forward to perform an Easter play. The pastor followed the children with a riveting message. His daughter sat with the team, quietly translating in order that men from the States could be a part of the service.

When the service ended, everyone began to stack the chairs against the wall to make room for steaming coffee and fellowship. Don turned to step outside to collect his thoughts and get a breath of fresh air. As he walked toward the rear door, a man stepped in front of him and blocked his exit. It was Checu!

"Do you remember me?" he asked, looking straight into Don's eyes. Of course Don remembered him. Checu had been the subject of many heated prayers Don had made over the years.

As uncomfortable as the confrontation was, Don sensed the Lord was in it. The men pulled two chairs down from a stack near the wall. They sat in a corner and began to talk. If there was one thing that Don had learned over the years as a pastor, it was that God places a higher priority on relationships than His children do.

It amazed Don how the issues between them seemed so much less significant than they had seemed years earlier. Don wrote this testimony:

> As I spoke with Checu, who had been wondrously
> used by the Lord in my absence, we realized that our
> feelings toward each other had changed. All the hos-
> tility was gone. We sat just a few feet from the stage
> where an empty tomb had been erected. The signif-
> icance was not lost on either of us as we bowed our
> heads and prayed. Together we asked God for fresh

mercies, and we received them in that upper room.
When we finished, we hugged each other, exchanged
e-mail addresses, and then walked out into the sun-
shine together. In the bright light, I pondered how
God had beautifully set me up. He had called me six
thousand miles away from home to mend a broken
relationship.

Don had thought the relationship with his former landlord was
beyond repair. He had left it behind him and moved thousands of
miles away. But God wanted both of His sons free from the burden
of unforgiveness.

The Un-neighborly Neighbor

Joanie enjoyed walking her dog every morning before going to
work. It was a special time for her to greet the morning and spend
time with her husband. Her dog, Bud, had been a rescue dog. He
also looked forward to the morning walks. Bud would wait near the
door, his tail wagging, barely able to hold still as Joanie fastened his
leash to his bright collar.

One morning, as Joanie and Ed walked passed a neighbor's
house, an aggressive dog came charging at her from the driveway.
Joanie ran to the middle of the street. The dog came at her full force.
While Ed stood in stunned silence, Bud took up the fight. Standing
in front of Joanie, Bud growled. Soon the dogs began to engage in
a vicious fight. Joanie tried to disengage Bud, but he was too strong.
She fell to the ground and splayed out on the asphalt.

The neighbor began to scream at both Joanie and her dog. He
hurled expletives at them. Joanie waited for over a minute pressed
down upon the street. The angry dog retreated and Joanie got up.
Joanie was crying so hard she couldn't speak as she turned to walk
away.

"What do you think you were doing, you crazy woman?" the
neighbor yelled after her.

Joanie screamed back, her body shaking with rage and shock. "What were you doing? Something's wrong with you!"

Joanie was mad! She was mad at her neighbor. She was mad at her husband, who kept trying to soothe her anger. She wanted to call the police. Her husband dissuaded her. "Honey, there really is something wrong with him. I think he's an alcoholic. I've watched him before. Why don't you forgive him and let it go?" Forgive him and let it go? Now Joanie felt betrayed by her husband too.

Just a few months later Joanie passed the same house on her morning ritual with Bud. The neighbor's dog came charging out again. Joanie jumped and crossed to the other side of the street. The dog charged at Bud. This time, Bud was ready and fended off the menacing dog. Joanie was shaken.

The neighbor looked on laughing, making an offensive gesture with his hand.

Seething with anger, Joanie recounted the ordeal to her husband. She demanded that Ed do something. Ed went to the neighbor's house and tried to reason with him. The encounter didn't end well.

Joanie chose a new route for her morning walks, but she still had to drive by the neighbor's house as she traveled to and from work. Every time she did, she felt the anger rise up in her.

Two years later, as she and Ed were preparing to retire for the evening, the doorbell rang. Ed answered the door. It was the neighbor and he wanted to apologize to Joanie. She refused to forgive him. In fact, she refused to go to the door. "Tell him to go away; I'm not interested," she yelled to Ed, who stood awkwardly in the open doorway.

A few days later, the neighbor spotted Joanie alone on her front porch reading the newspaper. He came up to her and formally asked if she would forgive him. Joanie realized that her Bible was visible on the table next to her. She secretly prayed he wouldn't see it. There was no way she was going to forgive this man.

She held the newspaper up and covered her face. "I don't see you, just like you didn't see me lying helpless in the street when our dogs were fighting."

He attempted another apology. Joanie continued to ignore him, silently willing him to go away. When she heard his footsteps retreating, she pulled the newspaper down. She glanced over at her Bible on the table next to her. It was a blaring and visible conviction to her actions. "Oh God," she prayed, "please don't let him know I am a Christian. You might be able to forgive him, but I can't."

A few weeks later, Joanie went with some coworkers to a Christian conference. She attended a special workshop on children's ministry. During the class, they showed a five-minute clip of a new video for kids on forgiveness. In the cartoon, a cat held a mouse tantalizingly over another cat's mouth. The little mouse trembled and quaked with fear. "Ugh," Joanie thought, "this is horrible."

Joanie felt the Lord speak to her heart. "Joanie, you are just like that cat. You are torturing another human soul in your refusal to forgive your neighbor. You need to tell your neighbor that you forgive him." Joanie burst into tears. She prayed and asked God to help her to forgive.

When Joanie returned home, she reported to her husband the story of the cat and mouse and what the Lord had spoken to her. Ed felt relieved. He felt so sorry for the neighbor and he had been disappointed in Joanie's behavior.

A day later, Joanie had the opportunity to put into practice the lesson the Lord showed her. She was sitting on her porch when the neighbor walked up to attempt another apology. Joanie visibly tensed. "Lord, not this soon. Can't I have a bit more time?" she begged silently.

The neighbor asked Joanie for forgiveness for how he had acted and what he had done. Joanie offered a very stiff forgiveness. The neighbor asked if they could hug. She slowly rose. The whole idea of a hug repulsed her. Joanie stood rigidly and let her neighbor wrap his arms around her. She waited for the ordeal to be over. He gently squeezed her arms. He turned and began to walk toward the sidewalk.

That's when everything hit Joanie. "Joe, wait!" she cried after him. Joanie ran down from the porch and threw her arms around him. "I forgive you. I forgive you," she cried. "I'm a bigger sinner than you are. Please forgive me."

Tears streamed down Joe's face. He could barely speak. He nodded his head up and down as they stood facing each other on the grassy lawn in front of Joanie's house.

Joanie savored the sweet release she felt in her body. Forgiveness felt good. It felt really good. She was free.

A few days later, Joe stopped by again. This time Joanie was glad her Bible was visible on the table beside her and that she had a Christian book in her hand. They helped her introduce her faith by saying, "Joe, do you know what I'm reading right now?" Joe looked at the book she now held up. It was a devotional by a well-known pastor.

"The author talks about how God has forgiven us for all our sins and wrongdoings because His Son, Jesus, paid for them on the cross. Do you know what that means? It means that you and I are forgiven for all the bad things we have done, if we choose to believe in Jesus."

Joe looked uncomfortable, but he listened. Joanie briefly shared her own testimony with him. "I'm not perfect. I still blow it. Jesus shows me every day how much I need Him."

Her neighbor looked at her with understanding as Joanie continued, "None of us are perfect. We are all progressing."

Joe stops by their house often now. Ed and Joanie continue to share the love of Jesus in words and actions with their neighbor.

All these stories reinforce the reality that forgiveness is not always an easy choice, but it is the right choice. Sometimes that choice needs to be exercised over and over toward the same person. Forgiveness as an attitude, mindset, and heart perspective is a daily choice that we must make toward every person who offends us. We do this because "God in Christ forgave you" (Ephesians 4:32).

Questions for Study and Personal Reflection

1. Read Luke 17:3-4. How do these verses minister to you about forgiveness?

2. What offenses do you find the hardest to forgive others for?

3. How do you see unforgiveness being a detriment to your relationship with others?

4. List some ways you can incorporate the practice of forgiveness into your daily routine.

5. Why do you want to forgive others?

Prayer

Dear Lord,

Thank You for teaching me how to forgive friends, strangers, and loved ones. Give me a greater sense of compassion toward others and a heart that is willing to take the steps needed to forgive and be free. Each time I face the faults and sins of another person, I am reminded of how human and fallible I am. When negative thoughts about my life and past rise up, help me to forgive myself and to grow in a spirit of grace. In Jesus's name, amen.

Chapter 13

Living a Story of Victory

Have you ever thought of your life as a story being written by God? We all know that the greatest stories present trials, challenges, and numerous perils that the main character must overcome. The adversities that the heroine faces only endear her to us. If our heroine becomes embittered by her circumstances, we lose sympathy. However, if she chooses to forgive her adversaries and press through each difficulty with grace, we cheer her every step. And when we watch her transform through this perseverance, we are inspired to do the same.

You are the heroine in your own story. And when you walk in God's forgiveness you are walking in and living out a story of great victory.

We have come a long way on this path together. We've explored what it takes to forgive, how to forgive, and even what misconceptions can keep us from forgiveness if we don't base our lives and decisions on God's truths.

As I mentioned before, forgiveness is an ongoing process. Not only do we sometimes have to keep forgiving the same person over and over, but we also encounter new situations, hurts, and people to forgive. The story continues. And for that to be a story of victory, you will need to be vigilant to protect your heart from unforgiveness.

The apostle Peter warns believers, "Be sober, be vigilant; because your adversary the devil walks about like a roaring lion, seeing whom he may devour. Resist him, steadfast in the faith, knowing that the same sufferings are experienced by your brotherhood in the world" (1 Peter 5:8-9). Satan is out there, wanting to devour Christians through unforgiveness. Satan knows the powerful hold that unforgiveness has on our hearts. He knows how unforgiveness can color every circumstance in deathly hues. He knows that unforgiveness can render a believer totally ineffective for spiritual victory. He knows that unforgiveness will not only terrorize the one who holds it, but all those who come into contact with it.

In 2 Corinthians 2:10-11, Paul urges the Corinthian believers to forgive lest Satan would take advantage of them, "for we are not ignorant of his devices." Let's face it; unforgiveness is one of Satan's greatest weapons against Christians.

I pray this chapter will inspire you and prepare you for your new life of forgiveness. We'll examine God's Word and we'll look at the stories of women who have chosen to be victors. Together, we can glean strength and encouragement for our continuing journeys.

Isn't it exciting to realize that *your* story is also being shaped to encourage others? Your walk as a woman who chooses to forgive is an example of what it looks like to hope and rest in God's strength, grace, transformation, and victory.

Will You Be a Victim or Victor?

The attitude that most often sways you from victor to victim is the attitude of blame. When we blame others for the disappointment of our plans or dreams, it's time to examine and guard our hearts. Recently, I was driving with my mother to church. We were running late, and I was going a little faster than necessary when a car swerved right in front of me and forced me to brake and slow down. The car continued to poke along in front of me, forcing me to reduce my speed to a minimum. My mother was upset by the delay and said, "Do you think the devil is in that car attempting to make us late for church?"

No sooner had she asked the question than we saw a policeman on his motorcycle with his radar gun pointed right at us to check our speed. Because we had been forced to slow down, we were in no peril of getting pulled over. Mom immediately turned to me and asked, "Well, do you think that there is an angel in that car, keeping us from getting a ticket on the way to church?" How quickly our perspective had turned from blaming the pokey car for making us late to blessing the pokey car for keeping us from getting a ticket.

To keep ourselves from routinely blaming others for spoiling our plans or ruining our dreams, it is essential to see God as sovereign over our circumstances and every person's actions. God is often saving us from an unforeseen tragedy through the change of our circumstances. God will use people in a variety of ways to keep us on the path that leads to the works of God being revealed.

Don't blame others for disappointing circumstances. Refuse to be the victim of your circumstances or of any person. That's what Paul did.

When Paul was in jail, he refused to blame anyone for his imprisonment. In the epistles he wrote from prison, he referred to himself as "the prisoner of the Lord Jesus Christ." Though Paul could have easily blamed the unscrupulous religious leaders in Jerusalem for inciting a riot against him or the corrupt Roman authorities in Caesarea for refusing to set him free, he chose neither. Instead he chose a higher perspective. He chose to see himself in the mighty hand of God. From this divine perspective, Paul could see God working in a myriad of ways. In Paul's epistle to the Philippians, he explained to the Philippians all the great things God was doing through his imprisonment. In Philippians 1:12, he said that the gospel was being spread. In Philippians 1:13, he testified that the "whole palace" had heard the gospel. In Philippians 1:14, Paul spoke about the brethren in Christ who had been emboldened by Paul's chains to "speak the word without fear."

Paul was not practicing divine optimism. Rather, Paul was seeing his circumstances through the eyes of God's purposeful plans.

God's Glory Revealed

Are you blaming someone or something for your disappointments? Stop! You are in dangerous territory. Rather, yield your disappointments, hurts, and hardships to God. Ask God to reveal His glory in them. That's what my friend Anita did!

Anita was only 28 when she was diagnosed with aggressive breast cancer. When the doctor came in with the diagnosis, Anita lifted her arms to God and said, "Lord, use my cancer for Your glory."

Before Anita turned 30, she learned she had ovarian cancer. Her hysterectomy destroyed her dream of being a mother. Later on lymph nodes had to be removed, and Anita had to wear ACE bandages to keep the swelling in her arms and legs to a minimum. I watched Anita endure surgery after surgery, procedure after procedure, and hardship after hardship. Yet during her entire ordeal, she always smiled and testified that her cancer was God's gift to her to showcase His glory and share the gospel with others.

Anita led many cancer patients to Jesus while sharing chemotherapy sessions together. Often the nurses at the hospital would ask her to pray for another patient who was struggling to come to terms with their cancer. Anita was always ready and took every opportunity given.

For over thirty years Anita allowed God to use her cancer for His glory. At her funeral the church was packed with people who testified of the glory that Anita displayed during her ordeal. I am sure that when she reached heaven, the doors were thrown open and a glorious crown was placed on her head. Anita was never a victim of cancer. She walked in victory and now she wears a victor's crown.

God Above All

Truly, it is your choice whether to be over your circumstances or under them. When you invite God into your hardships, He will reveal His glory. When you believe and live out the belief that God is more powerful than any trial or hardship you experience, you will enjoy His protection and comfort in new, transforming ways.

I don't know about you, but I hate feeling like a victim. The Bible assures me in Romans 8:31-39 that through Jesus I am more than a conqueror.

> If God is for us, who can be against us? He who did not spare His own Son, but delivered Him up for us all, how shall He not with Him also freely give us all things? Who shall bring a charge against God's elect? It is God who justifies. Who is he who condemns? It is Christ who died, and furthermore is also risen, who is even at the right hand of God, who also makes intercession for us. Who shall separate us from the love of Christ? Shall tribulation, or distress, or persecution, or famine, or nakedness, or peril, or sword? As it is written: "For Your sake we are killed all day long; We are accounted as sheep for the slaughter." Yet in all these things we are more than conquerors through Him who loved us. For I am persuaded that neither death nor life, nor angels nor principalities nor powers, nor things present nor things to come, nor height nor depth, nor any other created thing, shall be able to separate us from the love of God which is in Christ Jesus our Lord.

If you had any doubts about your status, now I hope you know—you *are* a victor. The cross was the great victory against evil. Jesus has secured the victory for us so that we don't need to be terrorized, tyrannized, or trodden down by people or circumstances.

Focus on Forgiveness

Where we direct our hearts, minds, thoughts, and actions is our focus. We can talk the talk about forgiveness, but if we are not choosing forgiveness with every part of ourselves, we will step off the path. We'll become distracted and uncertain.

When we focus on the triumph of Jesus Christ on our behalf over every authority in heaven and earth, we become victorious women who know that every person, circumstance, and hardship becomes fodder for God's glory rather than foes for our demise. God will turn each tragedy to triumph as Paul states in 2 Corinthians 2:14: "Now thanks be to God who always leads us in triumph in Christ, and through us diffuses the fragrance of His knowledge in every place."

Julia remembers the romantic notions she once held about her first husband, Paul. She had first heard about the dashing young soldier from her friends at work. Paul was handsome, and Julia was in love with love. On their first date they went horseback riding, and Julia, with her beautiful voice, sang out the lilting lyrics to "Ramona."

The romantic illusions vanished quickly after Julia married Paul. He was abusive, violent, and had a very dangerous side. No amount of love, understanding, or cooperation on Julia's part could pacify his malevolence. Besides his abuse toward Julia, Paul was also constantly in trouble with the law.

Julia didn't know what to do, and she was more concerned for their son's welfare than even her own. She sought out a Jesuit priest for counsel. She knew things were seriously wrong when he told her to absolve the marriage and get away from Paul.

Julia's only reprieve from Paul was when he went to jail. She felt broken and weary. It was a feeling she knew well from a history of strife, loss, and suffering. When she was nine, she had lost her best friend. When she was eighteen, her beloved sister died. In her twenties, she had to have a hysterectomy. Years later, her brother was killed in a flash flood.

There was great pain in Julia. She knew she had to move forward in life and do so in healthy ways. While Paul was incarcerated, Julia sought a divorce. She moved to a different town and worked as a checker at a grocery store. She worked hard to do a good job and be a valued employee.

In time, Julia met a wonderful man who was a widower and had a son from his first marriage. Phil and Julia soon got married and combined their two families. Julia continued working at the market but was available to help Phil with the records and accounting for the fledgling business he started.

It was around this time that Paul got out of prison. He called her and made plans to meet her for lunch. He claimed he wanted to make arrangements for visiting his son. Paul came to meet Julia at her store. He lingered about the aisles and watched the activity of the store employees.

At lunch Paul asked, "What would you do if I held up your store?"

Without hesitation, Julia answered, "I'd report you to the police."

Paul smiled. "What if I held a gun to your head?"

Julia was resolute: "I'd make sure with my last breath that you went to jail." Paul laughed.

A week later, a sister store across town was robbed. Julia was suspicious. It was eerily similar to the robbery Paul hinted about at lunch. Julia went to the police. The police did not trust Julia right away. Paul was investigated. The police soon discovered that he was the armed robber who held up the market. As soon as Paul was booked, Julia was brought under investigation as a possible accomplice. However, her supervisor testified to Julia's distrust of Paul and her integrity as a person and an employee. The investigation was dropped and she continued to work.

Years after emerging from these emotionally trying times, Phil and Julia met a man who was in town to preach at a motorhome lot near them. They had been impressed by his open and friendly demeanor. When Julia saw an advertisement for the preacher's faith rally, she convinced Phil to attend with her that night. While at the event, they were stirred by the invitation to give their lives to Jesus. Both Phil and Julia became Christians that night.

One of the first things God placed on Julia's heart was the need to forgive. Julia was so excited about her newfound relationship with the Lord that she was willing to give God whatever He required. She was even excited at the prospect of having something to give to Jesus that He wanted. She chose to forgive everyone who had hurt or injured her, including Paul.

Then one day, nearly twenty years after she chose to forgive Paul, he wrote her a letter to apologize for the injury and pain he had brought into her life. Julia was touched and began to pray for him.

By this time, both Julia and Paul were well into their 80s. Julia contemplated what a wonderful ending Paul's apology was to the long saga of suffering and triumph. However, it was not at all the end of the story. There were still more chapters to be written.

Paul called her just a few weeks ago and wanted to know how and why she became a Christian. Julia was able to explain everything to Paul. Before she hung the phone up she asked him, "Paul, do you want to become a Christian?"

It thrilled Julia to hear Paul answer, "I just might."

"Well," she answered, "you'd better do it soon. You might not have much time left to deliberate!"

Julia's once tragic tale has turned into an epic saga of victory. Had Julia not made the decision early on in her Christian life to forgive, her story would have ended quite differently.

Some people thwart the story of their life. They close the book when the story is only half written. In 2 Corinthians 3:2, the apostle Paul writes, "You are our epistle written in our hearts, known and read by all men."

If you stop your story in the middle of adversity, if the offender is able to continue to emotionally oppress, or if you hold on to unforgiveness, there will be no more chapters to be written. There will be no uplifting ending. When we choose to forgive, we are choosing to keep our stories of faith alive and eternal.

A Redemption Story

Cara's life is one of those that could have ended in defeat. Instead, it is a story of transformation and the victory found in forgiveness.

Growing up in a non-Christian home in England, the concept of forgiveness was never understood by Cara. Later, when she was a young woman, she became a Christian and read her Bible every day. One morning she came across Matthew 6:14-15, "For if you forgive men their trespasses, your heavenly Father will also forgive yours. But if you do not forgive men their trespasses, neither will your Father forgive your trespasses."

Cara knew and was thankful that the moment she received Jesus into her heart, God had forgiven all the bad things she had done. She was thankful that God continued to forgive every sin she confessed to Him. But the concept of forgiving others was new to her. She turned to God and asked, "Lord, is there someone I need to forgive?"

Instantly, the answer came to Cara. She needed to forgive her father. Her father? Her father had violated her, abused her, and left her suicidal. God wouldn't allow something buried deep in her past to put a damper on her future. God wanted Cara to walk in freedom and victory. Forgiveness came to her spontaneously. It was a natural and freeing step of faith. Her father and freedom were only a phone call away! Cara chose to forgive her father and walk forward in victory.

Cara's mother, Gladys, struggled to understand what Cara had done. Gladys could not forgive her ex-husband. She felt betrayed when Cara did. When Cara found out her mother was dying, she returned to England to be near her. She brushed her mother's hair, rubbed her aching back, and made her tea and sandwiches.

The last days of Gladys's life were quickly passing. Cara could tell there was something on her mother's mind. Gladys needed closure before she died. As they sat eating trifle together, Gladys suddenly said, "I understand you've spoken to your father."

"Yes?" Cara responded. It was more a question than an answer.

Mustering every ounce of strength left in her frail body, Gladys assumed a tone of authority and demanded, "Why?" Gladys had divorced Cara's father when she found out about the sexual abuse. She had loathed him for how he had betrayed her and violated their children. As far as Gladys was concerned, he had ruined all of their lives. Her hatred ran deep.

Cara explained that despite what had happened to her and the mistakes she herself had made, her life was far from ruined. She had found peace, freedom, love, and purpose in Jesus. Usually the mention of Jesus would move Gladys to anger. Now she listened, hoping to understand the reason for her daughter's unwarranted forgiveness.

Cara explained how she had been forgiven by Jesus Christ for every sin and wrong she had ever done. She had felt a sweet release when Jesus forgave her. She wanted her father to know the sense of that release too. So, at the prompting of God, she had called her father and forgiven him.

Deeper hurt lay below the surface of Gladys's questions. "Why did you write that you couldn't tell me about your father's abuse because we weren't that close? I still have the letter you wrote in my dresser drawer!"

Cara concentrated. She needed to think back thirty years. Her intention had not been to injure her mother, but to explain why she didn't want to tell her mother that her father had violated her. That letter had been the turning point in her mother's life. It was Cara's letter that made Gladys end the marriage.

Cara took a deep breath. "Mother, I was twenty and very immature when I wrote that letter. I am fifty now, and I want you to know that you have always been my friend."

Gladys's burden seemed to ease. She looked at her daughter and with deep regret in her voice said, "We could have all moved somewhere together. I was young enough then to have started over." Cara and Gladys both fell silent for a time.

A few moments later, Gladys spoke again, this time with a sob. "I didn't know. I didn't know." Cara took her mom's hand and held it. "I know, Mum. It wasn't your fault." Cara wanted to relieve every ounce of the condemnation her mother had carried. Cara longed for her mom to be free as she was free.

"Dad was evil. My sister and I knew what was happening to each other but we couldn't talk about it, even with each other. We were so afraid of him. He is the one to blame, not you. I made it right with him, but if he doesn't make it right before God, he will pay. He will go to hell."

Gladys seemed vindicated. "Good!" she said.

Cara tried to lighten the mood. "So, Mother, do you have any last words of wisdom for me? Last words are very important."

Gladys smiled. A mischievous look crossed over her face. "Yes, stop being such a Jesus freak!" Cara laughed. She knew her mother thought that she'd lost her mind in America when she had gotten saved.

The moment to say goodbye came sooner than either expected. Cara hugged Gladys tightly. She whispered into her ear, "Mother, you don't have to be afraid to die. Just call on Jesus's name and I will meet you again in heaven." Cara had done all she could. She exited the room, leaving her mother in God's capable hands.

On the flight back to America, God comforted Cara's heart with a promise from Luke 19:9-10: "Today salvation has come to this house, because he also is a son of Abraham; for the Son of Man has come to seek and to save that which was lost." Cara received a sweet assurance from the Lord that she would see her mother again and their story would continue in glory with no pains from the past to ever trouble them again.

Cara's story is still being written. Every chapter gets better and better.

One Last Story

A person would never know that Delaney had such a riveting testimony. She is a well-adjusted, thriving, and accomplished woman. She is educated, eloquent, and maintains a successful career. Delaney is married to a wonderful Christian man and they have three very loved and brilliant children. Nothing in Delaney's current life or demeanor hints at the rejection and depression she survived in the first part of her life. What I and others don't get a glimpse of is a past of pain and abuse. And worst of all, the deep wounds were caused by the person who should've loved her most: her mother.

When Delaney was born, her mother and father were convinced that the hospital had given them the wrong child. Delaney did not look like her brothers. It was only after her sister, who looked much like her, was born that her mother conceded that Delaney really was her child. Delaney remembers her mother introducing her to her new little sister saying, "Well, I guess you really are my daughter. Your sister looks like you, only she's much prettier. You are so ugly."

With frequent comments like that, it is no wonder that Delaney grew up feeling unloved and unlovable. Her mother's contempt for her grew with every hardship her mother experienced. She considered Delaney to blame for all that went wrong. According to her mother, when Delaney's father left her mother, Delaney was responsible. When her mother couldn't pay the bills, it was Delaney's fault they were broke. When her mother drank too much, it was Delaney who drove her to it.

Delaney's young heart was broken again and again. She didn't have an example of love in her life until one weekend when a family down the block invited her to church. Young Delaney sat in the sanctuary listening with rapt attention to the message that God loved her. When the minister gave the altar call, she ran forward without hesitation and gave her life to Jesus.

Feeling the love of Jesus was a remarkable thing for Delaney, but the problems at home did not ease up and she had to face human rejection daily. Her mother refused to be impressed by Delaney's stellar grades, good citizen awards, and outstanding achievements at school. Right after high school graduation, Delaney was ordered out of the house with the threat that if she didn't get her belongings out in two weeks, her mom would throw them out.

Delaney moved in with a friend, worked two jobs, and supported herself through college. After graduating she found employment at a large company and tried to put the past in the past. Still her mother's cruelty haunted her. Delaney made efforts to have a relationship with her mother, but she was rejected, criticized, and insulted at every encounter.

Delaney kept her focus on work and continued to do well. She was given the responsibility of acquainting new employees with the corporation. This was how she met Jim. He was kind and a good man. They became good friends. Both of them were dating other people at the time, so the friendship seemed secure and safe to Delaney.

The truth was that Delaney was scared of relationships, especially ones that had potential to last. She sabotaged every relationship she had when it became too serious. Deep in her heart, she didn't believe anyone could really love her. Yet when Delaney and Jim's friendship continued to deepen, they both had to admit that they were in love. Delaney set aside her fears and she and Jim were married.

Life was going well for a few years. Jim continued to be successful at work while Delaney settled happily into housekeeping and mothering. It was not until their first child was born that problems began to surface in Delaney's mind. Her complete adoration of her newborn daughter brought up significant questions: Why didn't her mother love her as she loved her daughter? What was wrong with her that her own mother couldn't love her?

Delaney sought counseling, but she realized that it was fruitless to try to understand her mother. Confused and depressed, Delaney didn't know where to turn. During her struggles, her husband was praying fervently for his beloved wife. At church one Sunday morning, Delaney's pastor spoke on forgiveness. Delaney recognized the core of her own condition in his message. She knew then that she needed to forgive her mother.

After the service, she sought out the pastor. "How can I forgive my mother?" she asked. Delaney wasn't ready to go into the detailed account of how mean her mother had been. She didn't want to justify her feelings she held in her heart toward her mother. No. She wanted to be liberated from those feelings.

The pastor was sympathetic. He sensed her pain and desperation. Gently, he said, "You need to choose to forgive. Will and action will follow that choice. God will help you."

Delaney wept as the pastor spoke. He laid a gentle arm on her shoulder and prayed. Delaney resolved that moment to forgive her mother. In prayer she gave her mother to the Lord. There was no immediate release, only a singular resolve to forgive.

Delaney's resolve was tested the next day. A disturbing memory came to mind. She remembered an incident of her mother's hostility. Instinctively Delaney found herself writing it down on the ledger of her mind. Suddenly it came to her. She had been keeping a hidden agenda of all the callous things her mother had ever said or done to her. With startling detail memories of her mother's brazen cruelty toward her came to mind. Delaney began to reckon one offense after another. She prayed, "Lord, I can't afford to live under the tyranny of these thoughts anymore. Please deliver me." She felt a sweet release.

Moments later another memory of her mother's abuse came to mind. Delaney delivered the thought up to God. For a year, her resolve to forgive was tested, and every day she gained greater freedom from unforgiveness. One day she realized that it was all gone. She felt liberated at last. Not only was she free to forgive, but she was free to lavish affection upon her children and husband without fear or doubt.

Her pastor could see the change in her and asked her to share her testimony on a television program. Delaney couldn't believe she had the courage to share her story, but God gave her the strength to follow through. She was able to tell a host of people the glorious release she had found in forgiving her mother.

Today Delaney continues to share her story. Her story has helped other women to be liberated from the torment of unforgiveness. Delaney lives happily with her adoring husband and her three amazing children. She and her husband gave up their successful careers to serve full time in the ministry. Her story is far from over. In fact, it continues to get more exciting.

What about you? What chapter are you living in the story of your life?

Keep Walking in Victory

This book is filled with stories of men and women who chose to forgive. The hurts, injuries, and suffering in their lives were replaced with healing and freedom when they made the crucial choice to "forgive our debtors."

Every good book contains an element of tragedy and suffering. The quality of the story all depends on how the main character responds to the adversity. The stories in this book are still being written. Each is far from over. However, those who have chosen to forgive will testify that every chapter is getting better and better.

Some people try to halt God's progression of their story in the middle of a chapter. They let resentment, hostility, and anger interfere with God's greater story of healing and forgiveness. The story of the person who refuses to forgive is a tragedy. There is no resolve and no happy ending.

God wants your story to be a story of victory. God wants to help you to overcome the adversity, pain, and injury you have endured. He wants to set you free to live the adventrue of life. Jesus said in John 10:10, "The thief does not come except to steal, and to kill, and to destroy. I have come that they may have life, and that they may have it more abundantly." Unforgiveness is a thief that will steal, kill, and destroy your story. Jesus desires that your life be an adventure. He wants to turn every tragedy into a triumph. He wants you to experience the abundant life He brings.

Whether or not your story ends in triumph or defeat depends on whether you will make the choice to forgive. It's time to get on the path to victory! After you have finished these chapter questions for study and reflection, set aside time to pray and work through the Forgiveness Action Plan at the end of this book.

Questions for Study and Personal Reflection

1. Where are you in your story of learning to forgive?

2. If you were to write your story right now, what would the ending be?

3. Are you letting God write a new story or are you trying to hold on to the old version of your tale?

4. What is your favorite Bible story? What problems did your favorite Bible character face? How were those challenges overcome?

5. What excites you the most about walking in forgiveness and victory?

Prayer

Writer of my life,

Thank You for the story You are creating through me each day. When I am discouraged by the pain caused by others or the trials I face, I will rest in knowing that my story is not complete—it is unfolding in Your time and in Your caring hands. Help me give myself grace to grow and learn so that I do not become discouraged by doubts or negative self-talk. Instead, fill me with Your truth and Your Word so I can be free from the pain and prison of unforgiveness. In Jesus's name, amen.

A Prayer for You

Friend, it is an honor for me to pray for you. Thank you for walking along this with me. May you be blessed as you walk forward in the steps of forgiveness so you can receive the gifts of God's freedom in your life. Your heart and future will be transformed by the power of His grace and by His strength when you choose to forgive others.

Cheryl

Dear Lord,

I know my sister has felt pain. It is not an easy choice to forgive. Pain mocks her and fear grips her. Lord, take my sister's hand right now and give her the strength to choose to forgive. Let her feel the sweet release that comes from choosing to forgive. Set her free from all the resentment, hostility, and grudges that threaten the beauty of the story of her life. Lead her into the path of glory, love, and victory!

Lord, You chose to forgive. Then You ratified that decision with Your life so that she and I can be forgiven. Let her fully receive the power of Your forgiveness that she might be able to forgive others. I pray this in Jesus's name. Amen!

Forgiveness Action Plan

Date:

To prevent unforgiveness from gaining a hold on your heart, I encourage you to return to this section of the book or make copies of this page to use anytime you feel tension between you and another person, anytime you feel the weight of shame, blame, or regret, and anytime you feel the constraints of a hardened heart.

Take heed of this warning in Galatians 5:1: "Stand fast therefore in the liberty by which Christ has made us free, and do not be entangled again with a yoke of bondage." Anyone who has struggled to be free of unforgiveness will testify that it is a heavy yoke of bondage. Once you are set free, don't allow yourself to be entangled again in it.

Walk through these steps to keep making the choice to forgive.

Starter Prayer

Lord, I give to You every part of my life so my story can be one of faith, integrity, healing, inspiration, and victory. I will seek Your guidance whenever I sense a divide between me and others or a stress within my circumstances. As I work through these measures to safeguard my heart, I ask that You reveal to me Your will for each day of my life. I pray that my weakness will magnify Your strength and that my daily choice to forgive others will illuminate Your glory forever. In Jesus's name, amen.

Go to God Immediately

Proverbs 17:14 advises, "The beginning of strife is like releasing water; therefore stop contention before a quarrel starts." It is much easier to deal with anger, resentment, and hard feelings when they first appear. If they have the chance to build and accumulate power, eventually they come rushing through your life wreaking havoc and leaving a trail of debris in your relationships. Go to God immediately, before the first waves of hard feelings become a flood of unforgiveness.

- What issue or problem is gathering momentum in your life because you have not dealt with it?

- How is forgiveness or a lack of forgiveness related to this situation?

- What is a new point of conflict you are experiencing with someone in your life?

- Bring long held unforgiveness and new feelings of resentment to God right now. Write a prayer to ask for His release and His leading:

Be Vigilant

Whenever you sense the tug of resentment, bad feelings, or lingering malignant thoughts about someone, present them to God.

Remember that unforgiveness is always lurking in the shadows and wants to have a dominant place in your heart. Unforgiveness is one of Satan's devices.

- What negative emotions have you experienced this week?

- How have these emotions influenced your attitude?

- Write a prayer asking God to guard you against any attitude that would lead to unforgiveness.

Recognize the Culprits

When you find yourself blaming others or feeling like a victim, submit your heart immediately to God. Ask God to come in and purge your heart. Take time to forgive the person and rest in the assurances of Proverbs 3:5-6, "Trust in the LORD with all your heart, and lean not on your own understanding; in all your ways acknowledge Him, and He shall direct your paths."

- Examine the last time you blamed someone or a circumstance for how you felt. When did this happen and how can you look at it in a new way?

• Today, do you identify more with a victim or a victor? Why?

• Is there a part of your heart or life that you have not entrusted to God? List those and pray to stop leaning on your own understanding so that God's truths and ways will become known to you.

See "All Things" from the Hand of God

You probably know Romans 8:28 by heart: "We know that all things work together for good to those who love God, to those who are the called according to His purpose." Let God have the disappointments and hurts to use for His purposes. Let God make something beautiful out of your circumstances. Memorize 1 Thessalonians 5:16-18: "Rejoice always, pray without ceasing, in everything give thanks; for this is the will of God in Christ Jesus for you." Let this remind you of the many blessings in your life and God's hand in those blessings.

• What situation or area of life do you need to see God working in or God's hand in?

• Reflect on 1 Thessalonians 5:16-18. List three things you are thankful for or situations in which you can see God's hand right now.

- How does it make you feel to realize that if God is still in control of these blessed areas, He is also in control of the areas that are your current troubles?

- You are called according to God's purpose. In prayer, express your desire to understand this purpose and to walk in it.

Remember Your Identity in Christ

You are a victor in and through Jesus. You don't have to be under the tyranny of any person or circumstance. Ask God for that divine perspective on the present events transpiring in your life.

- Live today by embracing your identity in Christ. Write down three changes or shifts that take place when you do this.

- Who or what do you feel incapable of forgiving right now? Approach the task by realizing it is in and through God's strength and power that this can be done.

Let It Go

I love the New Living Translation of Ephesians 4:26, "And don't
sin by letting anger control you. Don't let the sun go down while
you are still angry." It is always dangerous to hold on to anger. It is
better to get rid of it before the day comes to an end. In prayer, pour
out your heart to God. Give Him your anger, and refuse to hold
on to it.

- What anger do you hold today that you need to release
  before day's end?

- Tomorrow, reflect on how it feels to start the day without that anger dictating your thoughts and influencing
  your heart.

- What are common triggers for your anger? Write those
  down and spend time in prayer about these catalyst situations or people. Give those to God as well and ask for a
  new way to see them and walk through them.

Closing Prayer

I hope these steps and questions bring you into God's presence
and to His lasting peace each day that you go through them. Below
is space for you to write a personal prayer to the Lord. Share with
Him what you have discovered by going through today's action plan.

Cheryl Brodersen has been serving Jesus together with her husband, Brian, for over 30 years. The Brodersens have four grown children and four adorable grandsons. Cheryl is the daughter of the late Pastor Chuck Smith of Calvary Chapel Costa Mesa and his beautiful wife, Kay.

Cheryl hosts the show *Today's Faith* aired on HisChannel and she shares inspiring faith lessons and insights on her website graciouswords.com where a large audience of readers and listeners enjoy her popular blog, radio show, and podcasts. Cheryl currently teaches a women's Bible study at Calvary Chapel Costa Mesa. She has taught women's classes at the Calvary Chapel Bible College in addition to teaching seminars, lecturing, and sharing at women's conferences and retreats.

Cheryl's passion for Jesus and His Word are evident when she speaks. Her enthusiasm for things of God is infectious.

Visit Cheryl at
www.facebook.com/CherylBrodersen
www.graciouswords.com
See or listen to Cheryl at
www.HisChannel.com
To learn more about books by Cheryl Brodersen
or to read sample chapters, log on to our website:
www.harvesthousepublishers.com

Other Books by Cheryl Brodersen

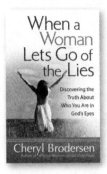

When a Woman Lets Go of the Lies
Author Cheryl Brodersen inspires you to embrace your extraordinary identity in Christ as you shed the big lies: "I'm not good enough." "God isn't strong enough." "I'm too flawed to be used by God." Encouraging, biblical guidance and inspirational illustrations will lead you to the comfort and absolute truth of God's power, promises, and blessings for you.

When a Woman Lets Go of Her Fears
Fear can be controlling and crippling. You want to trust God and experience release from the grip of fear, but how do you begin? Bible teacher, Cheryl Brodersen, knew this kind of fear but God spoke to her heart and took her on a beautiful journey toward freedom. With compassion, life examples, and biblical insights, Cheryl will help you find true faith and the peace that comes from leaving fear behind.

Growing Together As a Couple
Calvary Chapel Costa Mesa senior pastor Brian Brodersen and his wife, author Cheryl Brodersen, draw from God's Word and life examples to share ten essential "E" principles to help you entrust, encourage, energize, and endure as you embrace the wholeness of God's hope and plan for marriage.